LEICEST
celebrates

FESTIVALS IN LEICESTER PAST & PRESENT

WRITTEN BY VERNON DAVIS
with additional research by Narita Bahra

A LIVING HISTORY UNIT PUBLICATION

Acknowledgements

The Living History Unit would like to thank the many local people who generously contributed their memories and experiences to this book, including Mr M. Begg, Mrs K. Dorrell, Councillor H. Dunphy, Mr B. Francis, Rabbi A. Hill, Mrs Sharon Hood, Mrs A. Hussain, Mr A. Joyce, Mr Lam Luc, Mr G. Louis, Mr A.S. Matharu, Mrs R. Pankhania, Mrs B. Patel, members of the Chinese Community Project and the East West Project.
Thanks are also due to everyone who allowed us to reproduce photographs: Leicester Mercury, Leicestershire Museums, Arts & Records Service, Federation of Sikh Organisations Leicestershire, Guru Nanak Gurdwara and Sikh Museum, Polesie Dance Troupe, Pete Bryan, Stuart Hollis, Mrs S. Hood, Vasant Kalyani and George Wilson, Leicester City Council.

ISBN 0 9521090 6 9
© Leicester Council 1996
Published by Leicester City Council
Living History Unit
Designed by Creativity Works

CONTENTS

INTRODUCTION

Fifty years ago it would have been relatively straightforward to describe and explain the festivals celebrated in Leicester. Virtually all of them were at least nominally Christian, some with their origins in pagan practices.

Since the end of World War II, Leicester has emerged as one of the major multicultural cities of present day Britain, with a richness of traditions and customs. But if one major fact emerges from the study of its festivals today, it is that they are, by and large, evidence of the coming together of cultures over long periods of time.

The area of the city of Leicester, over the last two thousand years, has been settled by Celts, Romans - the Legions consisted of conscripts drawn from all over the Roman Empire, including North Africa, - Saxons, Danes and Norman French. These were followed by Jewish immigrants in the early medieval period. Others followed in the 19th century, refugees from economic hardship and religious persecution in Eastern Europe. In the last century as well as this, Italian immigrants settled in Leicester, and there has also been continuous migration from Ireland, Scotland and Wales.

The upheavals of the First World War saw Belgian refugees in Leicester, although most only temporarily, whilst after the Second World War numbers of European Volunteer Workers and refugees from several countries in Eastern Europe, notably Poland, Ukraine and the Baltic states, settled here. The late 1940s and 1950s witnessed the start of immigration from the Caribbean and from West Africa as well as from Gujarat, the Punjab, Pakistan and what was to become Bangladesh. Then came the Asians from East Africa during the late sixties and early seventies, whilst upheavals in South East Asia have resulted in Vietnamese people finding a home here.

Chinese immigration started with seamen settling in English ports in the early part of this century. In Leicester, in a similar fashion to the

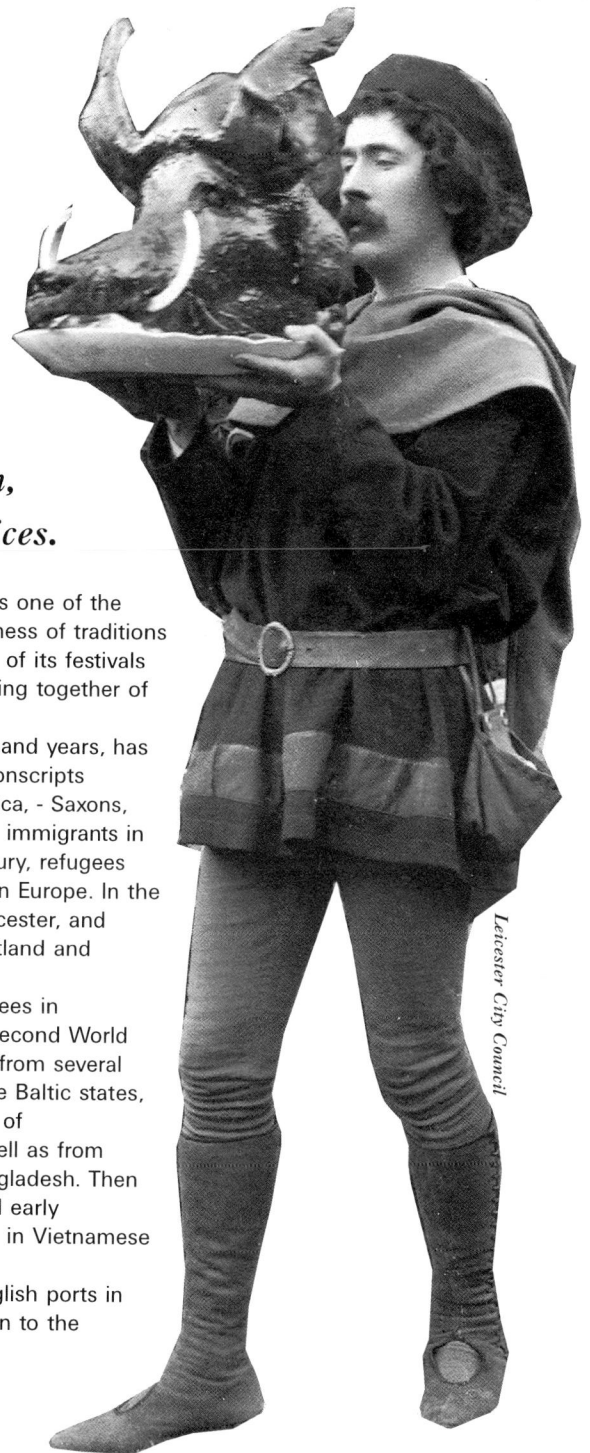

Diwali celebrations,
Belgrave Neighbourhood Centre
(Leicester City Council)

universal. It would be more surprising if we did not find points of similarity between all societies at different times. What may be more surprising is that similarities of belief, practice and origin are shared by the major religious groups.

Fundamental to all human cultures is the need to impose rhythm and structure on everyday life, whilst at the same time responding to the rhythms of the natural world. The events associated with these rhythms may be personal - transition from childhood to adulthood, for instance, or from the more carefree life of a single person to sharing the responsibilities of marriage or parenthood.

These transitions, in all cultures are marked by ceremonies, usually involving only family and close friends. The transition from life to death can however become the focus of a complex public ceremonial if the person involved is a great religious teacher or leader. In some circumstances, a funeral can also become a very public display of religious or political solidarity.

Other rhythms are universal. The transitions between night and day govern the working and sleeping pattern of our lives. There are other longer term rhythms. As modern humankind evolved as hunter/gatherers, living off the herds

Sylhetis from what is now Bangladesh, the Chinese occupied a niche in the restaurant trade. Each of these people have brought their own festivals with them. Two cultural groups may of course celebrate the same festival. For instance both the Chinese and Vietnamese celebrate the same New Year festival. Nevertheless, each culture has its own unique way of celebrating such festivals.

When one set of religious beliefs supplants another, there is often a reluctance to abandon favourite customs associated with the past, which then transfer themselves to the new circumstances - as for instance we shall see with Christmas.

However, it would be impossible to study the festivals of all Leicester's cultural groups without realising that they share certain similarities, such as the lighting of bonfires or candles, or the anticipation and excitement generated by the start of a New Year. This should not surprise us. The basic needs and emotions of the human race are of roaming wild animals, it is not too difficult to imagine the fear that the rains would not return, the grass start growing and the stock of prey animals be maintained. It was around these points in the year that festivals developed, but each cultural group living in Leicester today has developed its own calendar. A more detailed description of these may be found in the Appendix.

The words festival and feast have a common derivation, and special food is a feature of most festivals. There may be traditional ways of finishing up food prior to a period of fasting: this for instance is the origin of Pancake Day. Alternatively, for a culture which has taken root in a foreign land, food associated with the homeland may be eaten. Baked snapper, for instance, is a feature of the Carnival celebrations for Leicester's African-Caribbean communities. A special food may become identified with a festival due to its rarity or association with status. Imported tangerines and dates at Christmas are an example, while the association of nuts with Christmas is due to their seasonal availability.

A common theme running through many festivals is a suspension of the normal rules of society, or even a reversal of the roles that people normally fill. For instance, there is the custom in the Armed Forces for officers to serve other ranks at table on Christmas Day - just as the farmer served his employees at the old Harvest Home festivities. The Hindu Spring festival of Holi provides another example of the suspension of rules, with its tradition of people throwing paint or coloured powder over one another.

However all festivals are subject to evolution and change over time. Festivals which occur near to one another in time can become merged, while a festival celebrated by one group is often the occasion of a major event in another parallel cultural group. The martyrdom of Jesus took place at the time of the Jewish festival of Passover, whilst the Hindu festival of Baisakhi was the occasion for the founding of the Sikh Khalsa, now an important Sikh festival.

Perhaps the best example is the reintroduction of Christianity to England in the sixth century. Following the collapse of Roman rule and the Anglo-Saxon settlement, the Christian communities had been restricted to the "Celtic fringe" of Cornwall, Ireland, Scotland and Wales. In an attempt to reintegrate these fringe groups of Christians into the main body of the Catholic Church, and to convert the Anglo-Saxon settlers to Christianity, Pope Gregory gave explicit

Members of the Leicestershire branch of Comhaltas Ceoltoire Eireann (Stuart Hollis)

instructions to Augustine, who led the Christian Mission to these shores, as to how to deal with the pagan festivals celebrated by the Anglo-Saxons. These were quoted by Bede in his "Ecclesiastical History of the English People" completed in 731 AD:

"....because they are in the habit of slaughtering much cattle as sacrifices to devils, some solemnity ought to be given them in exchange for this. So on the day of the dedication or the festivals of the holy martyrs, whose relics are deposited there, let them make huts from the branches of the trees around the churches which have been consecrated out of shrines, and let them celebrate the solemnity with religious feasts. Do not let them sacrifice animals to the devil, but let them slaughter animals for their own food to the praise of God, and let them give thanks to the Giver of all things for His bountiful provision. Thus while some outward rejoicings are preserved, they will be able more easily to share in inward rejoicings".

Not only were pagan shrines taken over to be used as Christian churches, but also that pagan festivals, with some of their associated celebrations were combined with Christian festivals. Here we have a clear explanation of how some at least of the pre-Christian symbolism, such as the use of greenery for decoration, continues to this day to be associated with festivals such as Easter and Christmas.

Symbols of one sort or another form a major component of all festivals. Such things as candles, special clothes, bonfires and specific music all serve to define the festival and the way it is celebrated. However, the imagery associated with a particular festival may well change over time, and in the history of the festivals of Leicester certain major layers can be uncovered.

Undoubtedly before the Romans arrived, the Celtic people who lived here had a well established festival year, based around the agricultural seasons. The Roman occupation and administration of England and Wales, which lasted for approximately 400 years, saw the introduction of Roman rites and festivals. It should be remembered however that the Romans were principally town dwellers and their customs probably did not penetrate greatly into the countryside, where the native Britons would have continued to follow old traditions.

Most of the festivals which we celebrate in Leicester now, which

Eid celebrations
(Leicester City Council)

8

we consider to be traditional English festivals, are those that originated with the Anglo-Saxons, and in particular with their conversion to Christianity. Nevertheless, the actual festivals celebrated, and the manner of their celebration has changed greatly over the centuries. Major modifications came as a result of the Reformation, and the change from Roman Catholicism to Protestantism in the 16th century. This saw the end of many of the medieval religious festivals, and those festivals that survived were dealt another mortal blow in the mid seventeenth century by the Puritan Commonwealth under Cromwell. It was at this time that the celebration of Christmas, amongst other festivals, was abolished.

Following the restoration of the monarchy in 1660, Christmas and other festivals drifted back into the general culture, but they never regained their former importance until the mid 19th century. From then on, mass production of goods enabled manufacturers to exploit the commercial possibilities inherent in festivals, while other entrepreneurs offered entertainments to fill up the leisure time associated with a "holi(y)day".

Unfortunately it is not possible to cover every festival in a book of this size. However, it will be clear that the origins of many of the major festivals which are now celebrated in Leicester are rooted in the religious beliefs of the various communities, in particular the births of leading figures and their deaths - often as martyrs who died for their beliefs and ideals or their vision of universal truth. Hinduism and Judaism are the oldest of the religions considered here. Sikhism is the youngest, and drew on both the Hindu and the Muslim faiths at its inception. Judaism influenced, in different ways and at different times, both the Muslim faith and Christianity.

It is no surprise therefore to find parallels and similarities between the major festivals of all of these groups, even though the actual celebrations

Nilima Devi
(Leicester City Council)

may differ greatly.The three most recent, Islam, Sikhism and Christianity also share common features. All three owe their inception to what the founders saw as a deviation from the pure worship of a single God, and a preoccupation with ritual at the expense of worship and high ethical ideals. The birthdays and deaths of the founders of all three, Mohammed, Guru Nanak and Jesus are celebrated as festivals by the communities concerned.

The following comment by a Leicester person illustrates well this feeling of universality and identity of purpose amongst Leicester's different communities, a theme discussed at more length in the book:

"You may ask me to whom to pray - to pray to the Almighty God, whoever you are. If you are a Christian to Jesus, if you are a Muslim to Allah, if you are a Hindu to Krishna, if you are a Sikh to Guru Nanak... their way is only one way leading us to the same destination... their aims and objects are the same, universal brotherhood, love and peace... we are all the same, irrespective of any class, colour or creed, we are all the same... imagine different flowers in a garden - they look much better than all one type of flower, that is the beauty."

COMMEMORATIONS

Religious commemorations are at the heart of most of the major festivals of all of Leicester's communities. A common thread linking these festivals is the celebration of either the birth or death of the religion's founder, or some other decisive event in the emergence and growth of the religion in question. All the world's major religions are represented amongst Leicester's communities, and the knowledge that other followers throughout the world are celebrating the same event at the same time, reinforces the feeling of belonging, and enables individuals to gain from the support of all others.

Sikhs started coming to Leicester in the late 1940s. During the 1950s, Sikhs actually formed the majority of Indian immigrants who came to Leicester, and were the first substantial community of newcomers to the city. The Sikh homeland is the Punjab, an area of North West India.

The Punjab is now the name given to one of the States of modern India, but historically it consisted of a much larger area, a substantial part of which is now in Pakistan. Until the arrival of the British, the Punjab had provided the gateway by which all of India's conquerors had entered the sub-continent. Alexander the Great came this way in 327 BC, and so did the Mongols led by Mohammed of Ghor in 1187 AD.

This importance as a strategic routeway meant that the Punjab also became the meeting place of diverse

Demonstration of Sikh martial art Gutka, during Baisakhi procession (Federation of Sikh Organisations Leicestershire)

11

cultures and religions. Importantly, for the future history of the Sikhs, the Punjab became a religious frontier zone between Hinduism, to the south and east, and Islam to the north and west. The Muslim faith found its way into this area of North West India from around 1,000 AD, and was given a major boost by the foundation of the Mongol Sultanate of Delhi in 1206. From the first quarter of the sixteenth century, the area found itself incorporated into the Mughal Empire under Babur.

Guru Nanak, the founder of Sikhism was born into this religious and political cauldron in 1469. His father was a tax collector for the Muslim owner of his village of Talwandi, now known as Nankana Sahib. As a youth he came into contact with both Hindus and Muslims, and first found employment at the court of the Muslim ruler of Lahore, Daulat Khan.

Guru Nanak married at nineteen and within a few years two sons swelled the household numbers. It is quite clear that he had a deeply questioning nature, and by his thirties he was disillusioned by what he saw as the failings of both the Muslim and Hindu religions. In particular he despised the manipulation of what he considered to be pure religious principles for political ends, instanced both by Muslim/Hindu conflicts, as well as the internal rivalries and conflicts which affected both religions. He also abhorred superstitious ritual and the use of astrology.

Above all he wished his fellow men and women to experience the Oneness of God, and to live their lives according to the ethical code transmitted by God through himself. He taught also the potential equality of all men and all women before God, in antithesis of the Hindu and

Float carrying Guru Granth Sahib during Baisakhi procession.
(Federation of Sikh Organisations Leicestershire)

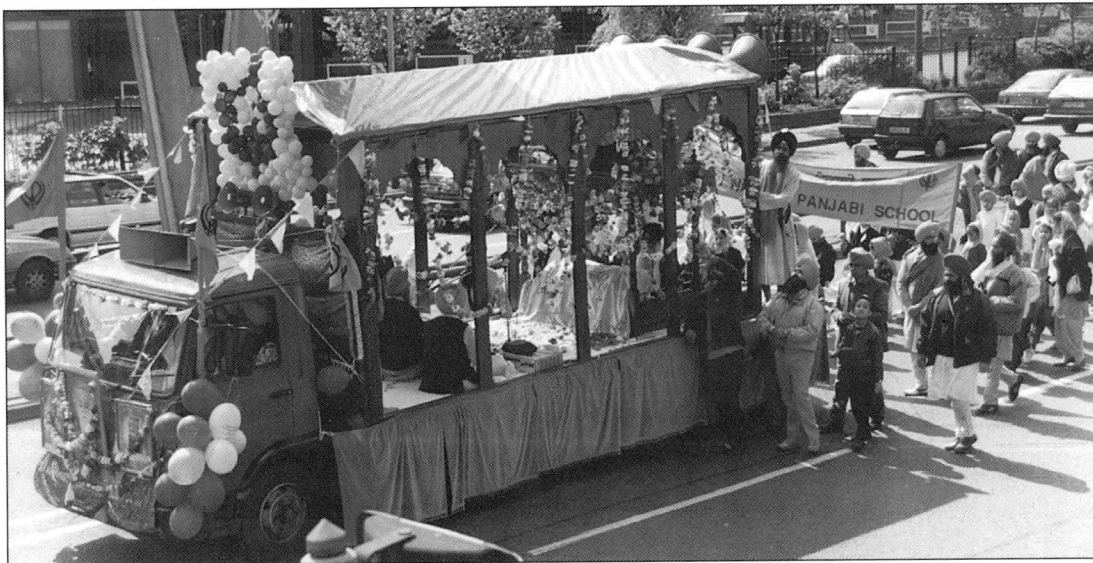

Muslim attitudes to women at the time, as well as the Hindu caste system, and the exploitation of the people by their Mughal rulers.

When he was about fifty years of age, Guru Nanak founded a small community of his followers. Under his leadership the small group, established at Kartarpur (now in Pakistan), prospered and grew. Towards the end of his life, Guru Nanak selected one of his followers, Lehna as his successor, and initiated him as the second Guru shortly before his death (or as Sikhs believe, before he left the Universe) in September 1539. In addition to leaving behind a community, Guru Nanak also left behind a collection of hymns, which became the foundation of the Sikh Scriptures now known as the Guru Granth Sahib.

The birthday of Guru Nanak is the principal festival in the Sikh calendar, and is celebrated generally in November/December, on a date calculated as per the Sikh calendar. The focus of the festival is the Gurdwara, or Sikh Temple. The major Gurdwaras in Leicester are at Holy Bones, near St Nicholas Circle, and in East Park Road, although there are others. Celebrations for the Guru's birthday begin the night before with fireworks, whilst greetings cards are exchanged between friends and families. Three days before the birth date of Guru Nanak, Akhand Path (non-stop reading of Sri Guru Granth Sahib) is started in the Gurdwaras. The bhog (termination) of this Akhand Path takes place after 48 hours, and then Diwan (Congregations) are held, and the devotees throng in heavy numbers to celebrate the day with great enthusiasm and inspiration.

From the early hours of the morning of Guru Nanak's Birthday, prayers are recited in the Gurdwaras as well as in people's homes. The Guru Granth Sahib is taken on a procession, or Nagar Kirtan, of the city on a decorated float, the followers singing the Shabads, the hymns of the Guru. Back home, the children hear stories from the Guru's life and candles are lit. Streets and homes are decorated for the occasion, new clothes are worn and sweets exchanged amongst friends and relations.

Here is one of Leicester's Sikh community talking about the significance of Guru Nanak today,

"Guru Nanak was a universal master. He loved every human being, he loved all creation and he showed us the way... and what you should do, and he reminded us, remember where you have come from, where are you supposed to go, and in between what are you supposed to do. He gave us a complete system, which if anybody, not only the Sikhs, but any person in the world who follows that system, he may be an individual, he may be family, he may be a small community, he may be a city, he may be a country or a nation, they are bound succeed. They must follow the rules of honesty, integrity, respect, fairness and justice. Guru Nanak gave us ten Golden Rules... and if you follow those rules, then you are far away, you love everybody, there's no hatred in your mind."

The fortunes of Sikhism during its formative years were inextricably intertwined with the ebbs and flows of political and religious thought amongst the Mughal rulers. For a great part of the life of the Fifth Guru, Arjan Dev, the Mughal Empire was ruled by Akbar in a spirit of religious tolerance. Akbar did not seek to turn India into an Islamic state. The Guru undertook travels throughout the Punjab and the numbers of Sikhs continued to increase. Many of those attracted were Jats, small landowning farmers. It was during the Guruship of Arjan Dev that work commenced on Harimandir, (Abode of God) popularly known as The Golden Temple, at Amritsar in the Punjab.

Guru Arjan Dev was also responsible for collecting together the hymns of the first three Gurus, together with those of his father as well as hymns of his own. He also collected nineteen compositions of the Hindu and Muslim saints, which were found to be in agreement with the teachings and ideology of Sri Guru Granth Sahib. These compositions were incorporated into Sri Guru Granth Sahib and form a significant part of the Holy scripture. Arjan Dev was not only the spiritual leader of the Sikhs but took an active role in their economic welfare as well as the political debates and intrigues of the time. It was his involvement in the politics of succession at the Mughal court which was to seal his fate, and in June 1606 in Lahore he was tortured to death on a hot plate heated from a fire below and with hot sand poured on him from above.

The Martyrdom of Guru Arjan Dev is universally commemorated by Sikhs. The day is marked in Leicester by gatherings at the Gurdwara. In addition to singing hymns appropriate to the occasion, special cold drinks are served. For children there is ice cream at school and at the Gurdwara.

The martyrdom of Guru Teg Bahadur, the 9th Guru, is equally commemorated with great enthusiasm and inspiration throughout the world. Sikhs in Leicester start the celebration of this day in advance, by starting a series of reciting Akhand path accompanied by the performance of Kirtan and Katha. The celebration attracts large numbers of people from all walks of life. In order to commemorate the significance of this date, Sikhs in Leicester have opened a Gurdwara in the name of Sri Guru Teg Bahadur in East Park Road.

The Birthday of the tenth Guru, Gobind Singh forms another important celebration in the Sikh calendar. Guru Gobind Singh is seen by Sikhs as combining all the best qualities of his predecessors. In addition to the foundation of the Khalsa, described in the next chapter, he made a fundamental contribution to the future of Sikhism, and one which has a major role to play in all the Sikh festivals celebrated today.

The lives of the ten Gurus encompass a period of around 200 years, from 1469 to 1708. During this time the body of written work grew and became known as the Adi Granth ("adi" means "first", "granth" means "collection" or "anthology"). Its origin lies in the hymns of Guru Nanak, but it was the fifth Guru, Arjan Dev who laid down its present structure. During the lives of the ten Gurus, Sikhism could be said to have two voices of authority, that of the scriptures, the Adi Granth, and that of the living Guru, although it would be more correct to say that both were serving unitedly as a medium of communication by God.

It had been the practice of each Guru to nominate his successor before he died. The major departure from this of Guru Gobind Singh was that he nominated the Holy Scriptures to be his successor, which were henceforth known as the Guru Granth Sahib. The importance of this act cannot be understated, and the Guru Granth Sahib, always identical in form, written in the Gurmukhi script and consisting of 1430 pages is to be found in every Gurdwara throughout the world, whilst readings from it form a mainstay of the celebrations at all Sikh festivals.

Judaism forms one of the oldest religious traditions in the world. The festivals of Judaism are rooted firmly in the historical experiences of the Jewish or Hebrew people. The symbols and customs of Jewish festivals reflect four thousand years of religious, cultural, economic and agricultural history.

The origins of the Hebrews are obscure, but evidence from archaeological finds, confirmed by narratives in the Book of Genesis, indicates that Semitic tribes started to settle in Palestine around 2,000 BC, and undoubtedly some of the festivals draw at least part of their inspiration from this period. Prior to their settlement in Palestine they appear to have been a nomadic pastoral people following their flocks from Mesopotamia to Syria. Of course, the Hebrews did not settle in an empty landscape, but amongst people who already lived there. Jewish culture even today owes much to the fusion of the cultures of these early people.

Following their enslavement by the Egyptians, the Jews regained their freedom under the charismatic leadership of Moses sometime shortly before 1,000 BC. They returned to their homeland, which was established as a unified Israelite kingdom by King David in 1,000 BC. Elements from the Jews' early history, their pastoral and nomadic beginnings, their settlement as an agricultural people and the Exodus from slavery in Egypt, all find expression in the celebrations of Passover, one of the main festivals in the Jewish calendar.

Passover is a spring festival which celebrates "first fruits". The first-fruits in question however are quite distinct and separate, drawn on the one hand from the Jews pastoral history and on the other from the agricultural settlement. According to the instructions in Exodus and Deuteronomy (see: Exodus, ch. 12, and Deuteronomy ch. 16), a lamb had to be sacrificed `at the going down of the sun' at the time of the full moon in the month of Nissan, when the barley was ripening. These two elements, the pastoral and the agrarian, are kept strictly apart in the celebrations of the festival even today.

Overshadowing the agricultural features of the festival, however, is the annual commemoration of the deliverance from slavery in Egypt, the Exodus, recalled in the name of the festival. The story related is that God instructed the Jews in captivity in Egypt to smear the blood from the sacrificed lamb on the door posts and lintels of their houses, so that when He smote the Egyptians with plague He would recognise the houses of the Jews, pass over them and they would be spared.

Celebrated in the western calendar in the period March/April, in the Jewish calendar Passover is celebrated from the fifteenth or sixteenth to the twenty first or twenty second days of the month of Nissan. Of major significance to Jewish culture is that the Passover is a family festival, and is celebrated within the home.

During the Passover, products made from fermented grains, i.e. leavened bread etc, are not allowed in the home. This means that products made from fermented grain, or from yeast, such as whisky or Marmite are also prohibited. During the period of Passover, only unleavened bread is eaten. This is seen as symbolic of the dough the Israelites carried with them at the time of the flight from Egypt. This dough was hardened in the sun to become matzah. Crucial to the manufacture of matzah is that there has to be less than 18 minutes between adding water to the flour and baking.

The first night of Passover, and outside Israel the second night, is the occasion for a service held in the home, called the "seder" service. Based around the family table, it re-enacts the Exodus of the Jewish nation from slavery in Egypt. On the table should be the shank bone of a lamb. This symbolises the "pesah" lamb, sacrificed at the time of the Exodus (see Exodus ch. 12.) Also present should be an egg, symbolic of temple sacrifices.

A special food known as haroset, made to have the consistency of mortar, is eaten at Passover. Haroset recalls the building and construction work that the Jews were forced to undertake for their Egyptian taskmasters. Haroset is often made from ground nuts, grated apples, cinnamon, and wine. Recipes vary with different Jewish communities around the world.

Also present is a bowl of salt water and some bitter herbs. These remember the salt tears and the bitter years of slavery. The meal ends with a prayer for all Jews to be re-united in a rebuilt Jerusalem, but more than this, it is a plea for a peaceful world for all.

Here is what the festival means for one of Leicester's Jewish community today:

"...Passover can be a hectic time for the housewife. The preceding fortnight she, and her spouse if he is co-operative, will spring clean the house very rigorously, to make absolutely certain that during Passover not a crumb of bread is to be found anywhere within the house. During the week of Passover we even make sure that anything which is derived from grains, such as whisky or other spirits fermented from grain is removed from the house. It will be locked up in an outhouse or the garage. Cakes are made, but from potato flour not wheat flour. Keeping up the Passover is difficult because of the need to buy special food. It is difficult in Leicester because the number of Jews is not sufficient to support a proper Jewish grocer."

The festival of Purim commemorates an episode during the Jewish exile in Persia in 473 BC, recounted in the Book of Esther (Esther ch. 9). The Jews were a small community within the Persian Empire, ruled at this time by Ahuerus (better known as Xerxes). The story tells of a plot by a Persian known as Haman to put the Jewish community to death, but which resulted in the death of Haman himself on a gallows intended for the Jews. The festival falls on the fourteenth day of the Hebrew month of Adar (February/March).

Historically this festival was marked by indulgence in wine and food, the swapping of gender roles and boisterous behaviour in the synagogue whenever the name of Haman was mentioned as the story was told via readings from the Torah. A traditional food at this time is triangular cakes, decorated with poppy seeds. The best translation of their Hebrew name is "Haman's Ears"! Purim is particularly liked by children as it is an opportunity to dress up.

A more sombre commemoration, marked on 30th April, is Yom Hashoah, a day of remembrance for all those Jews who perished in the Holocaust.

Islam is one of the world's great religions, its followers accounting for approximately one seventh of the world's population. The country with the largest Muslim population is Indonesia. The Muslim (the actual meaning is "one who surrenders or resigns him/herself to God") faith was established by the Prophet Mohammed, as a result of divine revelations through the Angel Gabriel. Mohammed was born in the Arabian city of Mecca, now in Saudi Arabia, in 570 AD. He was a merchant and travelled with the camel trains trading throughout the Arabian peninsula. Mohammed believed in a single God, and attempted to turn his countrymen towards God and away from the idols they worshipped.

In Mecca he met great resistance to his preaching, and in 622 AD he left Mecca and journeyed to Medina, another desert city, some two hundred miles north of Mecca. This journey is known to Muslims as the Hijrah, and is seen by them as being an event of great significance. In Medina, Mohammed became a great leader, both in his role of Prophet and as a leader of the people.

The leaders of Mecca saw a threat in his rising power and made attempts to remove him which led to armed conflict. At a decisive battle at Badr in the month of Ramadan, two years after his journey to Medina, the Prophet and his followers won a famous victory, although they were heavily outnumbered by the Meccan army. In the eighth year after the Hijra, Mohammed and his followers finally returned and gained control of Mecca.

The first task of Mohammed and his followers following their re-entry into Mecca was to cleanse the building there known as the Ka'ba by removing the idols. The Ka'ba is believed by Muslims to have been built by Abraham, and to be the first religious building in the world dedicated to the worship of the One God. It is actually towards this building that Muslims face when they are praying.

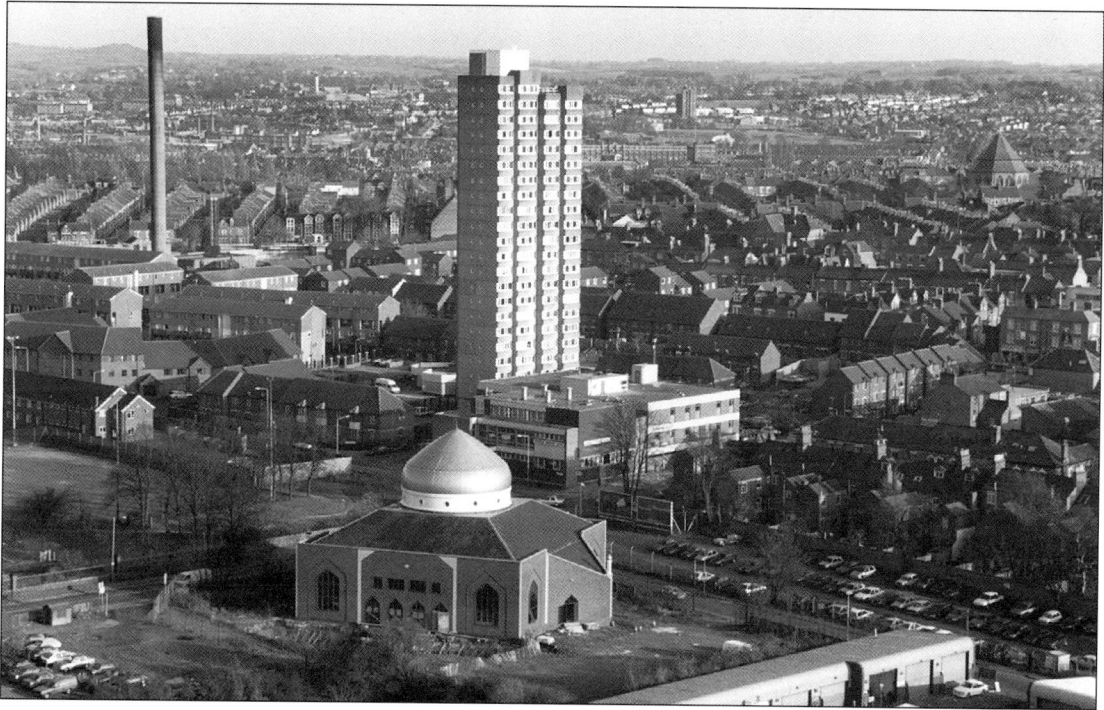

Conduit Street Mosque
(from "The Quality of Leicester", Leicester City Council)

In the years following the death of Mohammed, the Islamic faith spread across North Africa and the Middle East. Advancing as the Roman and Byzantine civilisations declined, Islam had spread to Spain by 712 AD, but another major expansion was eastward through Persia (Iran) and Afghanistan to the borders of China by 751 AD. Further expansion saw the conquest by peoples of the Islamic faith of those areas of the north of the Indian sub-continent now known as Pakistan and Bangladesh, as well as areas further south such as the Punjab and Gujarat.

Almost certainly the first resident from India to come to Leicester this century was Mahbub Alam, a Muslim from the Punjab, who started in business in Leicester as an eye specialist around 1922. His brother, who arrived here in the early thirties, is at the time of writing still alive and living in Leicester. From 1950 onwards more and more people from the Indian sub-continent settled in Leicester, many of them Muslims from Pakistan and what is now Bangladesh. It is reckoned that today the Muslim community in Leicester is some 25,000 strong.

Many of the Bangladeshi community have their family roots in the small inland area of Sylhet. Strangely, although hundreds of miles from the sea, Sylhetis have been arriving in England

and settling here for over two centuries, as it was from Sylhet in the eighteenth and nineteenth centuries that the British East India company at Calcutta recruited what were then known as "Lascar" seamen. The Muslims from Sylhet were considered more adventurous than the local Hindus, who at the time were reluctant to leave their homeland. The Sylheti Bangladeshis settled in the dockland areas of London and other ports and often worked in cafes. It is to these Sylhetis that we owe the phenomenal popularity of Indian restaurants in England today.

The most important date in the calendar for Leicester's Muslim community is Ramadan. The Muslim calendar, which is a Lunar Calendar, consists of 12 lunar months of 28 or 29 days, giving a year of 354 days. This means that in relation to the western calendar, dates in the Muslim calendar move back by 11 days every year. Ramadan is the name of the tenth month of the Muslim year. Fasting during the month of Ramadan is one of the Five Pillars of the Muslim Faith, and is explicitly called for in the holy book, the Qur'an,

"You who believe, fasting has been prescribed for you, just as it was prescribed for those before you, so that you may do your duty on days that have been fixed. Any of you who is ill or on a journey should choose a number of other days."
(Sura 2: 183-184)

Ramadan is the only month actually mentioned in the Qur'an. It appears both in the context of fasting, and also because it was in the month of Ramadan that the Word of God was revealed to Mohammed and set down in the Qur'an,

"The month of Ramadan is when the Qur'an was sent down as guidance for mankind, and with explanations for guidance, and as a standard (i.e. for judging between what is right and what is wrong)."
(Sura 2: 185)

Reading the Qur'an
(Vasant Kalyani)

Fasting during Ramadan for a Muslim means that no food or water passes one's lips between sunrise and sunset. It also means that you do not smoke and also that you refrain from unkind remarks and quarrels, during the hours of daylight. The original definition of the hours for fasting was from the moment it is possible to distinguish a white thread laid alongside a black thread until the moment that it is no longer possible to tell the threads apart.

The actual month of Ramadan starts from the moment that the new moon of the month becomes visible in the sky, until the moment that the new moon of the next month, the month of Shawwal is visible. For Muslim communities in countries where the moon is invariably visible this is very simple to accomplish. In Leicester cloud cover can present difficulties, although tables are published showing the times that the new moon rises above the horizon.

Fasting is an act of respect to God and to his Prophet Mohammed, but it also encourages self-discipline and hence steadfastness and respect for one's self. For Leicester's Muslim community during Ramadan, the day starts an hour before dawn. A light snack is eaten soon after rising. From then until the breaking of the fast in the evening there is no further sustenance.

In Muslim countries, the pace of life slows during Ramadan, and very often a nap will be taken during the day. For a Muslim in Leicester there is no respite. Whatever his or her job, a Muslim here has to continue to work at a normal pace without food or drink. Working in a hot factory, often doing heavy jobs without food or drink all day demands tremendous commitment.

The breaking of the fast in the evening is a family occasion. Immediately after sunset, the moment is marked by a light snack, often of dates, and a drink of water. It is traditional to ask friends or other family members to join together for this moment of breaking the fast. After a short break for prayers, the main meal of the day is enjoyed by all. After the meal, those who are able visit the mosque for prayers and readings from the Qur'an.

It is traditional to read a section of the Qur'an at evening prayers for the thirty days of Ramadan, the whole of the Qur'an thus being read during the month. Leicester has some fourteen mosques of which three, including the new mosque in Conduit Street are purpose built. During the month of Ramadan it is not unusual for around 3,000 worshippers to attend the Leicester mosques for evening prayers. How different from the Leicester of 1969, when the Islamic Centre would hire a room, so that Muslims could gather together for prayers. These days a thousand people can attend the new Mosque in Conduit Street, and even then some may be turned away.

It is believed that it was on the night of the 27th of Ramadan that Mohammed first received the Word of God, in the shape of the Qur'an, from the Angel Gabriel. This night is known as the Night of Power, or Leilat ul-kadr. In recognition of the significance of the latter part of Ramadan, Muslims offer extra prayers and enjoy additional readings from the Qur'an.

The final obligation of the month of Ramadan is to make a charitable contribution for the poor. This is known as Zakat-ul-fitr or the "charity of fast-breaking". The practice of giving alms for the poor is taken seriously by Muslims, and is seen as bestowing additional virtue. Ramadan is seen as a time which reminds the rich of their good fortune, whilst also enabling them to share the experience of poverty. Fasting emphasises the equality of all before God.

During Ramadan it is traditional to send food to the homes of the poor. In Leicester, money is collected in order to provide a meal for all the Muslim students at the city's Universities, who gather together to eat.

The sighting of the New Moon which signals

"Eid Mubarak"
(Vasant Kalyani)

the end of Ramadan and the start of Shawwal, also ushers in Eid-ul-Fitr, the Feast of Charity. Eid is a feast of thanksgiving, and is more meaningful and all the more enjoyable for all those who have faithfully kept the Fast. In Muslim countries, Eid-ul-Fitr is a public holiday, lasting for three days. For the Muslims of Leicester, Eid often falls on a weekday. In this case, some celebrations of Eid will be delayed until the following weekend.

Eid is marked by special morning prayers at the mosque. After prayers, family and friends will gather together for lunch, the first lunch for a month. This is the time to wear new clothes, an important tradition. Presents will be exchanged. For Muslims, the last few days of Ramadan can provide a great many shopping headaches! This is a time of great happiness in Leicester's Muslim community. All greet one another with "Eid Mubarak!", or "Happy Eid". Handshakes and embraces are exchanged. This is a time too for rebuilding and setting to rights any relationships which may have become troubled during the past year.

For those Muslims who have come to Leicester from East Africa or the Indian sub-continent, celebrating Eid here is not quite the same as it used to be. The English climate, as so often, has much to answer for! Here is one of Leicester's Muslim community remembering Eid as it was celebrated in East Africa when he was a child,

"Eid was celebrated on the open ground, the weather being very good over there and people used to gather in hundreds and thousands and it was a very unique sight to see all the people saying their prayers together in such a large open space".

Whilst drinking of alcohol and dancing have no part in the celebrations of Eid, special food does! Meat and rice dishes, such as Pilau or Biriani, and sweets are the order of the day.

20

Typical of these is shir kharma, made from milk, vermicelli, sugar, dates and nuts.

Leicester's Muslim community mark the anniversary of the birth of the Prophet Mohammed by special prayers, and a procession. This starts at the Islamic Centre on Sutherland Street and takes a route onto East Park Road, and then back onto Melbourne Road, ending at the new mosque on Conduit Street.

Within the present day Christian calendar, the most important festival besides Christmas, discussed in a later chapter, is Easter. It commemorates the martyrdom of Jesus by crucifixion, and his rising from the dead three days later. Easter in years gone by took precedence over Christmas, which was not celebrated at all until around the third century AD.

Easter as it is celebrated in modern times, however, is not a simple festival to explain, as it contains many, in some cases conflicting, symbols and images drawn from both Christian and non-Christian sources. The ceremonies of the church which mark the Easter festival have also undergone many changes over the years.

Until the reformation, Easter, or more correctly the whole cycle of events marking the Passion and Resurrection of Christ, formed the focal point of the Christian year. With the exception of Christmas, which is a fixed festival, and the Saints' days, virtually all the other events in the Christian calendar take their cue from the Paschal Feast, as Easter was known.

The sequence of feasts commences with Lent,

Muslim procession during the month of Muharram from the Mosque in Loughborough Road. (Vasant Kalyani)

Easter card 1921
(Leicester City Council)

The Crucifixion is commemorated on Good Friday, which is preceded by Maundy Thursday. The Resurrection, commemorated on Easter Sunday and seen as signifying redemption, was the single most important day in the Christian Calendar. Indeed it was the occurrence of the Resurrection on a Sunday that caused it to be set aside as the Holy day of the week, whilst Friday was a day of fasting in commemoration of the crucifixion. Fasting invariably meant abstention from meat and the eating of fish.

Following the events of Easter is Ascension Day, which occurs forty days after Easter Sunday. The Monday, Tuesday and Wednesday preceding Ascension Day are known as Rogation Days. The Seventh Sunday after Easter Sunday is Whitsun, and this marks the descent of the Holy Spirit upon the Apostles, fifty days after Easter. An alternative name is Pentecost. The origin of the name of Whitsun, a corruption of White Sunday is unclear, but is thought to refer to the white robes originally worn by those who were to be inducted into the church by baptism on this day, a sight which apparently impressed the Anglo-Saxons enough to give it the name.

Easter was celebrated as a festival by the early church before Christmas was even thought of as a festival. The early title of the event was the Pascha, or Mensis Paschalis. The word Easter is derived from the name of the Anglo-Saxon Goddess of Spring, Eastre or Eostre, April being known to the Anglo-Saxons as Eastor-monath. The probable derivation of Eostre is from a Sanskrit word meaning Dawn, hence Eostre-Monath is the Dawn-Month, heralding the summer. Other spellings include Ostara and Eastur, the name of Aurora, the Roman goddess of the Dawn has the same derivation. In Germany, altars dedicated to the Goddess Ostara were known until recently as Easter Stones.

Even before the advent of Christianity, the celebrations of this month included ideas of death

the first day of which is Ash Wednesday. The day previous, Shrove Tuesday (discussed further in chapter 6) was the day for being Shriven, or cleansed of sin. Lent was seen as the preparation for the events of Holy Week, the eight days commencing with Palm Sunday and ending on Easter Sunday. Lent lasts for forty days, culminating on Good Friday, the day of the Crucifixion. Lent commemorates the time that Jesus spent fasting in the wilderness. The Sunday before Easter is known as Palm Sunday.

and regeneration. In Greece, and countries influenced by Greek culture, the festival of Adonis, celebrated in the spring, marked his supposed death, rebirth the following day and ascent into heaven. In more northerly latitudes, the tensions associated with the switch from winter to spring are naturally greater, and the celebrations associated with Eostre-Monath consequently of great importance.

Associated with the goddess of Eostre was her favourite animal and attendant, the hare. The hare was a common emblem throughout the ancient world for love and fertility. It is from this source that we now draw the symbolism of the "Easter Bunny". The subject of the Easter hare in a specifically Leicester context is described in Chapter 6. The egg too, has long been a symbol of regeneration and re-birth, as until the explanation of cell division was brought forward, the mechanism of growth within the egg was inexplicable.

In medieval Leicester, Easter was the occasion for the great dramas of Passion week. Churches built before the Reformation still often provide echoes of the rituals which marked the celebration of Easter, such as the Easter Sepulchre, a symbolic recreation of Christ's tomb.

Ritual associated with the Easter Sepulchre consisted of the placing of the Sacred Host in the Sepulchre on Good Friday, and its return to the high altar on Easter Sunday.

In the Corporation records for the year 1478 is to be found an item regarding payments to players who were involved at the playing of the Passion Play the year before. Mysteries, as plays were known which illustrated major events of Jesus's life, were extremely popular. The Passion play took place on Palm Sunday, the Sunday before Easter. Palm Sunday commemorated the entry of Jesus into Jerusalem riding on an ass, when palms were strewn on the ground before him.

From other items in the accounts of the Corporation and churches in Leicester, and our knowledge of the events in other towns, we can guess at some of the other ceremony associated with Palm Sunday in Leicester in the medieval period. These ceremonies had developed from those in Jerusalem current by the 4th Century AD. In Jerusalem, a solemn procession took place from the Mount of Olives which entered the city in triumph.

In medieval Leicester, there were probably processions associated with the major churches of St Martin's and St Mary de Castro, involving a person representing Christ seated upon a donkey.

Open air Easter service in Leicester Market Place 1992 (Leicester Mercury)

Willows rather than palms were used to strew the ground before his passage. An interesting footnote to the proceedings, provided by the accounts for St Martin's in the years between 1544 and 1547, is that the payment to the person who played the "prophet" at the reading of the Passion on Palm Sunday also include an allowance for ale!

Today there are differences in emphasis in how Leicester's different communities celebrate Easter. For instance there is a significant number of Catholics in Leicester, many of them from the Irish and Polish communities. In the following description of the Easter celebrations by one of Leicester's Polish community, some echoes may be discerned of how Easter was celebrated in Leicester during the medieval period.

"The celebrations start the weekend before, with a gradual build-up to the events of Good Friday and the days following. On Palm Sunday, we have the whole of the betrayal in church. That is said by the priest and two others re-enacting the betrayal of Jesus, Peter denying God three times, and Judas... Maundy Thursday is kept as a Holy Day. Good Friday we have the Stations of the Cross. That is the path that Jesus took. We have the Girl Guides and the Scouts every year, that is a tradition in Leicester... they go round saying the prayers. On Easter Saturday we go to church to bless our offering. The offerings are an egg, which signifies birth, a piece of bread, meat, salt and pepper for spice, and cake for the fact that it is something sweet. All that is put into what we call a koschaka basket. Usually decorated with greenery and flowers, and the paschal lamb, which again the Girl Guides in Leicester (I can only talk about Leicester, because they are our Leicester traditions), the Girl Guides make and sell for the money that they need to buy things. The paschal lamb, that is put there, and we all go to church and it is blessed. All the food is blessed by the priest at the ceremony, and that is called the 'Blessing of the Eggs'.

On Easter Sunday we have breakfast and the eggs that are blessed, one of them is cut up, sliced, and before you have anything else to eat, you have a piece of this blessed egg, hard boiled egg, and you wish each other joy and happiness. On Easter Saturday night we have the resurrection, where you have all the readings, and then the unveiling... because we have a tomb in the Church, and it's covered by the rock, because that's where Jesus was buried. It starts at seven, and at about nine o'clock when you've gone through everything you get the bells pealing, and the stone is rolled away and it is an empty tomb, with just the cloth draped where Jesus was.

Before then we have a Cross laid out in front of the tomb, and people go up there and kiss the Cross as a gesture that Jesus died on the Cross. That is there until the Saturday, and on Saturday we have the Guides and Scouts standing guard over the tomb, they take it in turns to keep guard... There is nothing in the Church, all the flowers are taken away from the Church during Lent. There is no dancing goes on, all the statues are taken out, there is nothing, the Church is literally bare, because that is Lent, leading up to Easter when Jesus died. Then on Easter Sunday the whole thing is just a mass of flowers, everything is brought back, all the statues, because it's re-birth. That is how we celebrate Easter. Easter is far more important to us, religiously it is far more important because you've got far more to it, more involvement in it than Christmas."

The Easter lamb for the Polish community is represented by a table centre-piece of a white lamb on a bed of fresh greenery. The greenery is supplied by cress, sown especially for Easter on a bed of clay, smeared on stretched linen. Easter eggs, known as Pisanki are painted by the children. An essential part of the Easter meal are the traditional cakes known as mazurki. These consist of a flat pastry base spread with apricot or orange jam, or with vanilla cream. This is topped with dried fruit and nuts, or sometimes with the inscription "Alleluia". It is very important to the Polish community that these traditions of Easter are passed on,

"I've kept the traditions going even though I've got an English husband, and I think he would find it would be strange not to have that. My daughter stood there one day and said, - we were in the kitchen at Easter and doing the eggs - `when I have children of my own, I'm going to do exactly the same as I've had done to me. Thursday we'll go and buy the coloured pencils and the coloured felt-tips, (it's the only time we ever get new felt-tips in this house!), and on Friday we'll sit in the dining room and paint the eggs."

In Leicester, the Polish community sees the observance of Easter in the traditional manner as a way of keeping alive Polish traditions, and maintaining the integrity of the Polish community.

For many, Easter represents more of a holiday than a holy day, particularly for workers to whom it was, and is, an excuse to break the routine of their normal working days, whilst for children it represents two weeks of freedom from the discipline of school. Here is someone talking about their childhood Easter in Leicester before the first world war,

"We always had certain foods at Easter, our grandfather was a butcher, and he always used to hang, for so long before Easter, for Easter day, a joint of Welsh lamb, always was Welsh lamb, and it was always a very large joint. Sometimes it was a whole leg, boned and opened out so you could stuff it right through. So we had say stuffed lamb, new potatoes, because there was nearly always some in but they were very small, they're the dickens to scrape! Sometimes if it was a good year we might get peas as well. So on Easter Day what sweet did we have? Apple pie I think, with cream! Apple pie saved over the winter, you know, keeping apples. Certainly we always, every Easter

Sunday, we had stuffed lamb. Absolutely gorgeous."

Easter is perhaps always recognised as the first "day out" of the spring, and for many of Leicester's citizens this may take the shape of a trip to Bradgate Park, usually nowadays by car. Here is the story of an Easter Monday Day out more than seventy years ago when walking was the mode of transport for most, and which didn't altogether go as planned, due to that English weather!

"... my sister and I got up very early and we decided as it was a lovely sunny morning we would walk to Bradgate Park. We then lived at the top of Narborough Road, so it was quite some walk. We went across the fields to Anstey and then into Bradgate Park... opposite to the ruins. We went in lovely spring frocks, no coats - Father advised us not to do it but we took no notice - just before we left Anstey... it started to snow. At first just a few flakes, and then it REALLY snowed... so we went down into the Park... to the first big oak tree, we stood right tight to the bole and we ate the food our mother had packed us up, and by this time it was snowing and blowing good and proper, a blizzard! So... we turned round and walked back all the way to Leicester in the snow, blowing and snowing all the way. Then we had to walk from the corner of Groby Road up to the top of Narborough Road to get home.

When we got in, and got nice and warm and had something to eat and drink, we decided that as we'd now changed and got warm, we'd ask our Father what was on at the Palace, which was the variety house. We said we thought we would go there. He said well all right then, told us what was on, and so we had our food, got dressed and walked down then to the Palace in Belgrave Gate. When we get there we have to wait in a long queue because we had only got sixpence each to get in the gods (the upper circle), and twopence each to buy a quarter of sweets from the shop next door... got a reasonable seat... and then came out after an evening... of tip top variety... and walked all the way home, and that was our Easter Monday outing!".

Easter bonnets are reminders of a tradition of wearing new clothes at Easter, here is an elderly resident of Leicester remembering Easter in the countryside early this century,

"We didn't have a lot of luxuries... the only egg I think I can remember having, and it was a luxury as well, we had an egg each for our breakfast, a new laid egg from the farm and mother's home made bread, because normally we couldn't have an egg each. That was our Easter treat, a boiled egg from the farm. We went to church on Easter day, it was quite a day, we went to church three times. Did we wear anything special? Well as special as we could! It was a saying that you must wear something new on Easter Sunday... it was supposed to be lucky... but all we got was a new hair ribbon!"

Of immense significance to Hindus is the incarnation or avatar of Vishnu, known as Krishna. For many, the date of his birth, on the eighth night of the dark half of Bhadrapada, is as important as Diwali. The festival in Leicester is celebrated in the period of August/September and is known as Janamashtami, or Krishna Jayanti. The pivotal theme of the festival is the story of the Birth of Krishna as the avatar of Vishnu.

The story relates how the demon king Kansa is told that he will be in mortal danger from the eighth child of his sister Devaki. He locks Devaki and her husband in a dungeon. Seven children are born to Devaki and Kansa kills them all. Devani becomes pregnant again, this time with Krishna. In order to protect Krishna when he is born, a miracle occurs and the guards fall asleep. Devaki's husband steals baby Krishna away and leaves Him in the care of a herdsman and his wife, Yashoda, far away in Gokul.

Another baby, in reality a goddess in disguise, is brought back and left for the guards and Kansa to find. When he attempts to kill the baby, the goddess appears in its stead and laughingly tells Kansa that his destroyer, Krishna, has already been born and will cause his doom.

The time of Krishna's birth is believed to be midnight and many Hindus will fast until midnight, and then welcome the baby Krishna in a cradle (or Paaranu) with singing, prayers and dancing. A statue of the baby Krishna is washed with a mixture of yoghurt, ghee, honey, sugar and milk (called Panchamrut). A statue or picture of Krishna will be placed on a swing which is rocked in turn by all the devotees, and offerings of gifts such as money, food, etc. are made.

Once again, celebrations in Leicester are more restricted than would be the case in east Africa or India. Because Lord Krishna's birth is marked at 12.00 midnight, celebrations, including a feast following the day's fast, would take place after that at the Temple. Hindus in Leicester find that due to the weather, and other restrictions on late night celebrations, the festival has to be curtailed, although a few temples still celebrate on British time at 12 midnight.

Devotees at Shree Sanatan Mandir, Weymouth Street,
celebrating the appearance day of Lord Krishna
(Vasant Kalyani)

FRESH STARTS

The human concept of time encapsulates two contradictory elements. The ceaseless repetition of the cycles of the agricultural year possesses a quality of timelessness. In contrast, the need to impose some order upon this never ending stream of continuity, the need to separate one cycle of events from another, calls for a beginning and an end. The desire to number these packages of time inevitably means that one cycle has to end and another begin. In nearly all cultures, this end and beginning is celebrated as a New Year Festival.

In these northerly latitudes it seems natural to start the New Year shortly after the Winter Solstice, when the hours of daylight start to lengthen once again, heralding a new growing season. However, the actual day from which different cultures have reckoned the start of their New Year is quite arbitrary. It should be appreciated that for cultures which developed nearer the equator, the solstices did not have such great significance as they do in the UK or anywhere else in northern Europe, America or Asia. Of course, the impact of science and technology, with heat and light readily available, means that even for people in the northern latitudes the solstices no longer enjoy the same significance as they once did.

The Winter Solstice achieved this greater significance in the north as a result of the fear that winter might not turn into spring. Bonfires, a common element in many wintertime festivals may be seen as an encouragement to the sun to provide the warmth which will initiate the next agricultural cycle.

New Year Card c1920
(Leicester City Council)

The situation regarding the start of a New Year can be made even more complicated by different institutions in a country starting their new year on different dates. In the Leicester of Anglo-Saxon times, before the Norman conquest, the Church started its New Year from December the 25th. The Anglo-Saxon state calendar however, used January 1st as the start of the New Year.

From the fourteenth century onwards, until the adoption of the reformed Gregorian calendar in 1752, both church and state reckoned the start of the New Year from March 25th, also known as Lady Day, or the Annunciation of the Blessed Virgin, this being the day commemorated as the time when the Angel Gabriel appeared to Mary telling her she was to be the mother of Jesus. However this date was not necessarily general amongst the population at large.

We find Samuel Pepys for instance in his diary in 1662 celebrating New Years Day on January 1st. Different national institutions within a country beginning and ending their year at different times may seem an absurdity which the modern world would have avoided. Not so, in Britain today there are at least two major institutions within the country which start their years at differing times to January 1st.

As described above, church and state in medieval England started their year on March 25th. This was also the Exchequer's day for reckoning the start of the new tax year. The devastating thought that they would lose eleven taxable days when the calendar was changed in 1752, is believed to have led to the start of the new tax year being moved forward by eleven days to April 6th. In 1752, the Government decreed that henceforth the New Year should commence on January 1st. The Inland Revenue still starts its year on April 6th.

The British education system starts its new year at the commencement of the autumn term, usually at some time in September, although in Leicester it starts in the latter half of August, due to the summer holidays starting earlier than for the rest of the country because of July fortnight. The rhythm and divisions of the academic year owe their origin to early monastic life, as it was in the monasteries that education was centred until the foundation of independent schools from around 1500 onwards. The effect of this is that the education system has three calendars running simultaneously, the financial year (commencing in April), the academic year, and the state calendar year. It leads, needless to say, to confusion and complication.

The British New Year festival is almost exclusively a secular festival, but for other cultures the New Year celebrations can have a religious significance. The Jewish New Year festival, Rosh Hashanah, falls on the first day of the month of Tishri (September/October), and as with so many festivals it is composed of several elements. The agricultural year in Israel depended for its fertility on the autumn rains. In common with Sukkoth, which falls later in the month, there is an echo of the tensions induced when the early farmers awaited the start of the rains. These are exemplified by the ceremony of Tashlikh, when pleading prayers are said beside a source of water such as a spring or brook. Very often at the same time, people will empty out their pockets, symbolically ridding themselves of the burdens of guilt of the year just ending. A special event of the day is the blowing of the shofar, a ram's horn, called for in Psalm 81,

"Sound the horn on the new moon, at the appointed time, on the day of our solemn feast...".

In keeping with other New Year festivals, many of the common symbols of starting afresh may be encountered, such as the wearing of new clothes. On the eve of Rosh Hashanah it is traditional to eat apple dipped in honey, the combination of sharpness and sweetness being seen as representative of the extremes of human experience.

Following Rosh Hashanah, and celebrated on the tenth day of the month of Tishri, comes Yom Kippur, The Day of Atonement. The period between Rosh Hashanah and Yom Kippur is seen as a time of preparation, of heightened spiritual awareness and self-examination. Here is how one of Leicester's present Jewish community sees this,

"...we believe that the Almighty sits in judgement on all mankind and we symbolically believe that He opens His book of life, or His ledger if you like and all our deeds both good and otherwise during the past year are reviewed during the ten days of penitence, and during those ten days we try and feel repentant generally, try and promise to lead a better life and be kind to other people, and this culminates with the tenth day, the Day of Atonement, which is a fast lasting for approximately twenty five hours from sundown on the ninth day of the New Year and terminating roughly an hour after sunset on the tenth day."

It is a custom for Jewish people to ask one another for forgiveness on the eve of *Yom Kippur*, in order to put right any wrongs or hurt between them. Yom Kippur itself is seen as a time of expiation between man and God. A time to set straight and agree an account of the sins of the old year, and then to draw a line beneath them in preparation for the New Year. Amongst the synagogue ceremonies and Torah readings of the day may be found memories of the "scapegoat", which received the sins of the people and was then dispatched alive to -

"a land not inhabited: and he shall let go the goat in the wilderness."

A key feature of Yom Kippur is the fast. The meal before the fast begins is a festive occasion with candles, whilst the food itself is wholesome and filling to build up strength for the twenty five hours of the fast. During this time nothing is eaten or drunk, a mark of self-discipline, and a willingness to concentrate on the spiritual rather than the bodily needs of mankind. Neither may any work be done. Apart from sleeping, the whole period of twenty five hours is devoted to prayer.

The complexity and variety of Hindu calendars leads to the New Year being celebrated at different times in different parts of India. The main Hindu New Year celebrated in Leicester is Diwali. Diwali is celebrated throughout India as a festival, but is specifically a New Year festival in Gujarat, an area of India which was once the homeland of many of the Hindu residents of Leicester and their families.

Gujarat is the state from which many Indians emigrated to East Africa. East African coastal states such as Kenya have been host to Gujarati settlers since at least around 1300 AD It was from East Africa that many of Leicester's Gujaratis came in the 1960's and 70's.

Not all of India celebrates Diwali as New Year. As we shall see, the Punjab celebrates the New Year at a very different time. The state of Gujarat however still adheres to a way of reckoning the years which has fallen into disuse in other parts of India.

Diwali is best thought of as a combination of festivals, in a similar way to Christmas and New Year. The festival can vary in length, but it always includes the New Moon day of the month of Kartikka. This normally falls at the end of October in the western calendar. A common feature to the celebration of the festival everywhere is the lighting of lamps in small earthenware bowls, known as divas or deeps. These are filled with oil and given a cotton wick. Diwali is an abbreviation for deepavali, which means row of lamps. In the evening, when lit, they are placed in rows both inside and outside houses. More and more nowadays they are being replaced by small electric lights or candles. Here is how one

Diwali celebrations
(Leicester City Council)

Leicester Hindu remembers Diwali during her childhood in Kampala, Uganda:

"...what I remember most is the lighting of the little divas, we couldn't wait, morning and night we used to light up the whole of the house, inside and outside the house, the whole house actually glowed with little divas, and we used to look forward to lighting all these hundreds and hundreds of little divas. All along the window shelves, doorsteps, the front of the houses and everywhere else. Every house, wherever you looked, all lit up with divas. Every time one went out we couldn't wait to run and light it up. People would all be visiting. All varieties of sweet dishes would be cooked as well, certain dishes that people just do at Diwali time. You exchange those, whatever you cook, exchange with your neighbourhood, your family, your friends. You have a great big tray, silver or stainless steel, and you have all these different varieties of food. Before Diwali, you clean everything, the floor, linen, everything. On the doorstep, you paint patterns, Rangoli patterns. This is a big occasion for children and they look forward to doing it..."

In India, the celebrations may include various local or regional rituals and meanings. Certain themes and stories however occur throughout India. The first of these is the defeat of the demon king Mahabali by the dwarf avatar of Vishnu. Vishnu is the Hindu God of benevolence. His appearance on Earth is as one of his avatars, probably best described as an incarnation. Yet another avatar of Vishnu is Rama, a God-Prince best known as the central character of the Ramayana epic.

Featured at Diwali is Rama's victory over the evil demon Ravana. The festival celebrates the return of Rama and his wife Sita to Ayodhya (a city in northern India), after Sita's abduction by Ravana. The lighting of the lamps is symbolic of the welcome given to the returning Rama. The lights are also lit to guide the Goddess Lakshmi, who is representative of good fortune and wealth. All the doors of the house are left open on her night, the third of Diwali, so that she may be encouraged to enter!

This night is of particular significance to businessmen. This, the third day of Diwali is the traditional day for the closing of the year's account books. Many businessmen will take their new account books for the next year to the temple on this night in order to take part in Lakshmi puja (an act of worship)

For those Leicester Hindus who can remember Diwali in East Africa or in India there is the inevitable sadness and regret that the celebrations are not the same as they were.

"...families are now segregated a lot, they live in different parts of the country. People lose touch with each other, so there is not the family joy there. It is each individual household celebrating, we now just stay in the house in celebration, and do the best we can. The children have to go to school, and the parents to work, so there is no feeling of Diwali. We do try to make up for it. On the next day is the New Year's Day, we exchange "Happy New Year" and on that day we touch the feet of the elders, to get a blessing from them..."

Leicester City Council, in conjunction with the Hindu community, is responsible for the largest display of Diwali lights outside India. The whole of Belgrave Road is lit up for the occasion, and

Mr Narandas Adatia and family taking part in Diwali prayers (Vasant Kalyani)

Hindus come from all over Britain to see the intricate displays. In the city's schools, children will be drawing and colouring Rangoli patterns, and listening to or re-enacting the stories of Diwali.

Sikhs celebrate Diwali as the day when their sixth Guru, Hargobind, was released from prison in the 17th century. When he reached Amritsar, Guru Hargobind was welcomed back by the overjoyed Sikhs, who held a candle-lit celebration at the Golden Temple.

In Gujarat, Diwali is the festival celebrating the New Year. In the Punjab, the Sikh homeland located in northern India and which used a different calendar, the New Year was celebrated on the day that the sun entered the zodiacal sign of Mesha or Aries, a day known as Mesha Sankranti. In the western calendar the date usually falls around April 12th.

In the Punjab, New Year was celebrated at the Hindu festival of Baisakhi, alternatively spelt Vaisakhi. It featured thanksgiving for the barley crop then on the verge of being harvested, and was thus originally also a 'first fruits' festival. Particular significance attached to the grain harvest. Being primarily farmers, the Sikh communities needed the cash which was realised from the sale of the grain to provide capital for the purchase of houses, pay for weddings or buy land.

Sikhs originally marked this day by listening to the teaching of the Guru, but also with Bhangra dancing, visiting family and friends and the exchange of gifts. Sikhs continue to celebrate New Year on this day, but subsequent events have enormously increased the significance of the festival for Sikhs.

The most notable event occurred at the Baisakhi gathering in 1699. At the time Sikhs felt themselves to be under political and religious pressures, from both Hinduism, and more

particularly from their Mughal rulers and Islam. The tenth Guru, Gobind Singh, realised the need to re-affirm the faith of the Sikhs. Sikhs had gathered with Guru Gobind Singh as had become customary at Baisakhi, at Anandur. The Guru spelt out to them the difficulties and hazards of the times they lived in, and emphasised that they needed to be strong, dedicated and united in their loyalty to their Guru.

He then requested, with his sword drawn at the ready, for a volunteer to come forward who was prepared, literally, to give his head for the Guru. From the hushed and fearful assembly one man stood forward. The Guru led him into his tent, to re-appear shortly afterwards alone, his sword dripping with blood. He asked for another to give himself in the same way, and eventually another stepped forward. Once again the gathering saw them disappear together into the Guru's tent, from which shortly afterwards only the Guru emerged, once again with his bloody sword.

Three times more the same scene was repeated. After the fifth volunteer had disappeared into the tent with the Guru, the Guru emerged with all five alive and well. The five were given amrit, a solution of sugar crystals in water, stirred by a sword in an iron bowl while reciting five Sikh prayers. The Guru himself was then initiated in the same way, followed by thousands who had witnessed the whole scene. From henceforward the five were known as the Panj Pyares, the Beloved Five.

A code of discipline was also announced by the Guru. From then on a new Brotherhood of Sikhs, to be known as the Khalsa (Pure Ones) would wear five symbols of their faith and determination (the Five Ks) - Kesh: uncut hair, Kangha: a comb, Kara: a steel bracelet or wrist guard, Kirpan: a sword, and Kachh: short breeches. All the initiated men would henceforth take the name of Singh, meaning Lion, and it was

Baisakhi procession 1986
(Federation of Sikh Organisations Leicestershire)

from this time that the tenth Guru was known as Guru Gobind Singh. In order to re-affirm the equality of women, they too could be initiated, whereupon they took the name of 'Kaur', meaning Princess.

From around the turn of this century onwards, pressures and events engendered by the cultural re-awakening which led eventually to the freeing of the Indian sub-continent from British imperial rule gained more and more momentum. The British, ever mindful of the captive market for exports and the tax revenues which India provided, viewed this development with some alarm. From the eighteenth century onwards, the Sikhs had congregated at the Golden Temple at Amritsar in order to celebrate Baisakhi. In the absence of any Gurus after the tenth, the Golden

Temple had become a focal point for their faith.

With a total disregard of the traditions and customs of others, the British Lieutenant Governor of the Punjab decided that the gathering of Sikhs at Amritsar for the Baisakhi festival of 1919 was connected with the movement for Indian Home Rule. He ordered General Dyer, the local commander, to prevent and break up the assembly of Sikhs who had come for their usual festival. General Dyer carried out this instruction by ordering his troops to open fire. The death toll was three hundred and thirty seven men, forty one boys and a baby. Opinions of course differ on the exact chain of events, but for Sikhs an extra dimension of meaning was added to the importance of Baisakhi.

The celebration of Baisakhi is a significant

Nishan Sahib Sewa
(Guru Nanak Sikh Museum)

cultural event in today's Leicester calendar. In 1986, a major initiative saw the setting up of a working party to co-ordinate many of the activities. The working party consisted of leaders from the various Sikh organisations within the city, together with officers from the City Council. Aiming to educate and inform, an exhibition was mounted at the Ramgharia Board Sikh Temple in Meynell Road, Leicester. The exhibition moved from there to the Guru Tegh Bahadur Gurdwara and finally to the Guru Nanak Gurdwara, then situated in New Walk.

It was estimated that six thousand people, half of them children, had visited the exhibition. It gave the visitors a chance to learn more of Sikh culture, religion and art. In order to create some of the traditional excitement of Baisakhi in the Punjab, street bunting was put up in the East Park Road area, as well as in New Walk, and a seven day funfair was set up in Victoria Park.

A special women's event was held at De Montfort Hall which was attended by the Lord Mayor. In 1986, Baisakhi fell on a Sunday, and on that day, organised by the International Sikh Youth Federation, a procession took place from the Meynell Road Temple to De Montfort Hall. Leading the procession were representatives of the Beloved Five, barefoot and holding drawn kirpans or swords. Following in the procession was the Holy Scriptures, the Guru Granth Sahib. Approximately seven thousand turned out for the procession.

A special cultural night on 6th May was the scene of traditional dancing and music. Music was by top Punjabi band Apna Sangeet. Far more wished to attend the event than could be accommodated such was its popularity. Of course, whilst all the various activities were going on, there was also a continuous recitation of the Guru Granth Sahib in all the Gurdwaras. The celebration came to an end with a Sikh Sports Festival held in Victoria Park which attracted teams from all over England.

On Baisakhi Day a ceremony of changing the clothing of the Nishan Sahib, the pennant which flies above the building, takes place outside the Gurdwara. But important events take place inside as well, as described by this long time Sikh resident of Leicester,

"...Baisakhi brings me back into real life... Baisakhi reminds me that you have to be a religious person, helping the people, the poor and the needy... religion is a personal thing between you and Almighty God... universal brotherhood, love for humanity and honesty and sincerity, that's what religion is. On this day it reminds us of all the history, all those who sacrificed their lives, and what we should be doing towards that end, to help the community and the people. So that's how it brings us back into life... we sing hymns in the Temple at the top of our voices to Almighty God to help humanity as a whole and to help us all so we can work together."

*Hockey match during Baisakhi Festival
(Federation of Sikh Organisations Leicestershire)*

An important part of the Baisakhi celebrations in Leicester now is the Sports Festival. Sporting prowess is held in high regard by the Sikh community, who have traditionally been leading competitors in wrestling and hockey, and harks back to the earliest Gurus who promoted physical fitness as befitting warriors -

"The Tenth Guru said you are not only a saint, you are a saint and a soldier, you've got to be physically fit. Any Sikh who is not physically fit is not following the Guru's instructions!"

In 1994, the Sports Festival took place over two days, and included hockey, football, badminton and table tennis as well as special events for children.

Many of the Sikh community in Leicester can of course remember celebrating Baisakhi in the Punjab. Here is one such talking about his memories of Baisakhi in his home area of Ludhiana in the Punjab,

"As young people whenever there was a festival we went to the temple and we cleaned and we organised and we decorated and we prepared for the march they do through (the village), singing hymns and all that, and we rejoiced and enjoyed all that. In India... people spend the whole day, and sometimes the whole week on the festival... they set up their tents and camp where they want to spend the night... and the beauty of the Sikh system with a festival is you have a free kitchen, free meals which was introduced by the Gurus."

On 17 June 1995, the Federation of Sikh Organisations and Affiliated Groups held the first Baisakhi Mela in Leicestershire, at Victoria Park. The organisers said "This is an opportunity for families to get together, listen to devotional music by top Asian Bands in a local park, encouraging young people to learn about their culture through a new activity".

China's modern governments have made many attempts to destroy the old cultural heritage of China. The New Year festival was renamed Chun Jie, the Spring Festival. Formerly it had many names such as Yuan Chen, the Time of Beginning; Yuan Shuo, First Day of the First Month; Yuan Zheng, Beginning of the First Month. Perhaps the most poetic of these names is Yuan Dan, the First Morning of the Year.

Connected with the festival are many familiar elements marking the start of a new cycle. Preparations commence around the twenty third day of the last month. This date was associated with the return to Heaven of the household God, the God of the Furnace, or the God of the Kitchen. His journey was undertaken to make a report on the affairs and conduct of each member of the family during the past year.

As we might expect, this was a time of additional chores for wives and mothers. Food needed to be prepared for several days ahead, so that no cooking was required for New Year's Day, whilst the whole of the house and linen had to be cleaned, a custom still observed today. It is traditional for the house to be decorated with lanterns, coloured paper streamers and flowers. This is the time for the children to be letting off fireworks - the loud bangs and flashes were believed to frighten away evil spirits. The household God was welcomed back on New Year's Eve. His return would be celebrated by a special family meal, whilst at midnight everyone should change into new clothes.

The Chinese New Year falls each year between the 21st of January and the 20th of February. It is the end of one of the traditional accounting periods for Chinese businesses and shopkeepers. It would be considered a loss of face if all outstanding debts were not paid before the start of the New Year. Failure to settle outstanding accounts could also be reckoned to bring bad luck in the coming year. The Chinese New Year is best

Chinese New Year celebrations
(Leicester City Council)

known in Leicester for the Lion or Dragon dance. The Lion or Dragon, a fantastic, giant, coloured mask worn by one person, with several others underneath his body, dances from home to home and shop to shop. The Dragon's mission is to frighten away evil spirits and bring good luck to the premises he visits. A gift of money to the Dragon results in good fortune for the coming year.

The small Chinese and Vietnamese communities in Leicester suffer from the same problem that affects Sikhs, Muslims and Hindus in celebrating their festivals. Whilst striving to keep their traditions and culture intact, they are faced with the problem that the Chinese New Year, which in their homeland would see general celebrations with people taking time off from work and shops and businesses closing, is here just another working day. This means that a nearby Saturday or Sunday has to be chosen for the celebrations.

The Vietnamese community, which consists of about fifty families in Leicester organises a celebration with traditional food. Dishes are cooked that have associations with good luck and prosperity. Typical is New Year's Cake made from rice flour and sugar. A family party is also likely to be held when the children will be given "lucky

Chinese New Year procession (Leicester Mercury)

money", small amounts of money wrapped in red paper.

The festivities in 1993, to welcome the Year of the Cockerel, took place at the Home Farm Neighbourhood Centre at Beaumont Leys. The story of the Vietnamese New Year was told to the children, whilst members of the Vietnamese Association Youth Club performed the Dragon Dance, and further traditional dances were given by the Vietnamese-Chinese Cultural Friendship Association.

Leicester's Chinese community is larger than the Vietnamese. Celebrations are however similar, reflecting China's influence for millennia over South East Asia as a whole. Traditional foods once again feature, such as sweet rice cakes and roast pork. A feature of the family celebration would be a speech by the father reviewing the family's fortunes over the preceding year, and Leicester's Chinese community still keep this tradition alive. The Chinese community in Leicester is large enough to utilise De Montfort Hall for celebrating New Year. In China, the New Year festival lasts for fifteen days, and is a time for visiting relatives and friends.

The festivities in Leicester for 1993, the Year of the Rooster for the Chinese, included a performance of a play telling the story of the Chinese New Year, as well as traditional dances and songs. Participants included pupils from Leicester's Chinese School, as well as members of both the Leicester Malaysian and Phillipino Societies, whose cultures share features with the Chinese. Many of Leicester's Chinese restaurants also have their own special festivities.

For Christians, the New Year celebrations form part of the Christmas holiday season, but the significance of New Year has declined as Christmas has grown in importance. One feature of New Year in Leicester used to be celebrations in Town Hall Square.

Most of the features now associated with the New Year celebrations are Scottish, or at least northern, in origin, from whence comes the name Hogmanay. The "Happy New Year" greeting though probably derives from the Romans. This Scottish influence is because New Year is celebrated to a greater extent north of the border than in the south. Far less importance attaches to Christmas in the north as a result. Christmas was abolished in Scotland by reformers of a similar persuasion as abolished Christmas in England. In Scotland however the festivities transferred themselves to the celebration of the New Year and there they have stayed. Thus from Scotland has come the now common practice of joining hands in a circle and singing Auld Lang Syne.

Becoming more commonplace now in the south and midlands of England is the Scottish, or north British custom of "first footing". The ceremony originally called for a dark stranger to knock on the door at the stroke of midnight and be invited in to the party taking place inside. He brought with him originally a bough of kindling for the fire and a sprig of mistletoe. It is more usual nowadays for a member of the party to leave via the back door, to knock, and re-enter through the front.

The gifts he brings now are more likely a piece of coal, some salt and bread. The dark stranger of course represents the coming year. The fuel for the fire recalls all the associations of midwinter festivals with fire and warmth and the rebirth of the sun. The mistletoe played its role of defying death by remaining green through the winter. Salt and bread are symbols of good luck and hospitality. Whoever the dark stranger is, and whatever he carries, he must be offered a piece of cake and a glass of ale to ensure good fortune for the coming year.

New Year's Eve in Town Hall Square 1989
(Leicester Mercury)

For Leicester's Polish community, New Year is a secular festival, marked by dancing and singing at the Polish Club. Here is a Leicester resident of Polish origins describing a traditional custom of the New Year celebrations,

"At midnight we have an old man with long flowing hair, grey hair and dressed in white. And then we have a young lady, a young girl, a virgin nine or ten year old, who comes in following the old man. That signifies the old year going out and the New Year coming in."

The New Year has become a time when national and local leaders issue messages looking forward to the coming year, usually along the theme of hopefulness for better times to come. For New Year 1915, shortly after the outbreak of the First World War, the Mayor of Leicester, Jonathan North, issued a typically patriotic assessment of the likely course of events,

"In the face of these uncertainties, it is a matter for profound satisfaction that we are able - being fully assured of the righteousness of the cause - to look forward to the future with hope and confidence.

Are we downhearted? Surely not. We need to be patient, steadfast and confident, fully assured that we shall emerge from the conflict not only triumphant but with a truer exemplification of those qualities by which alone a nation can be great."

How different, in comparison, was Jonathan North's mayoral message for New Year 1918,

"The times through which we are passing are the most tragic of any in the history of the world. The dawn of the new year fails us for the fourth time as a harbinger of peace.

We are all in perfect agreement in our desire, in our intense yearning for the advent of peace to the distracted and distraught Nations of the world; hence our deep sorrow and disappointment at its long delay.

Our disappointment is immeasurably increased

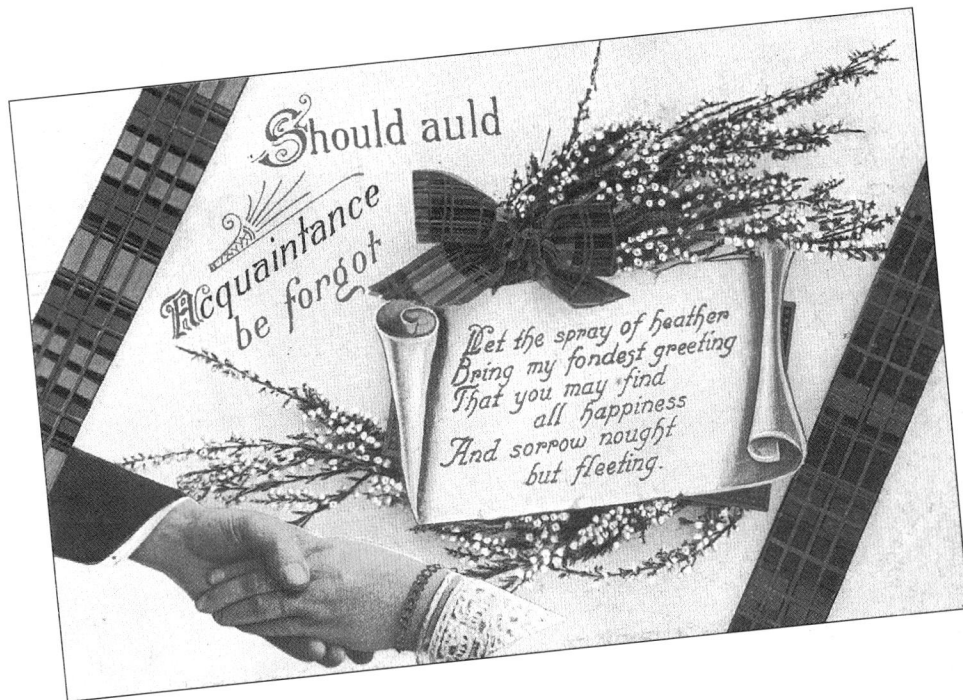

*Should auld
Acquaintance
be forgot*

*Let the spray of heather
Bring my fondest greeting
That you may find
all happiness
And sorrow nought
but fleeting.*

by the failure to discern the conditions necessary to a permanent and satisfactory peace, apart from which the deluge of blood, the sighs and tears, the broken hearts,the desolated homes and the indescribable agonies endured will have been in vain".

It would be easy of course to find similar worthy or sad, upbeat or gloomy prognostications at almost any New Year. Businessmen generally do not greet the New Year with a great deal of optimism. The hosiery industry has been a mainstay of Leicester manufacturing for some three hundred years. The following comment at the start of a New Year comes from a Leicester hosier named John Kirby who traded in Cank Street, where he also lived. Having started in the hosiery trade shortly beforehand, at the beginning of January 1816 he recorded,

"On a review of the state of my affairs I find that while my property is diminishing, my family is increasing, I am therefore making progress towards Bankruptcy which is a galling idea and calls imperiously on me for greater economy, and self denial in all the luxuries of life. I am therefore most resolutely determined in the present year to retrench every avoidable expense, to study and practice the most frugal methods of housekeeping."

John Kirby's difficulties were compounded by the slump which followed the end of the Napoleonic Wars. If the foregoing strikes a note with any present day businessmen, take heart, James Kirby continued to trade, with some ups and downs, until his death over thirty years later. What the quotation does show, however, is the need which we all feel to take stock once a year, learn from our mistakes and face a new year with optimism, hope and good intentions.

THE SEASONS

Seasonal festivals fall into two main groups, those associated with the solstices and equinoxes, and those that are connected with the main events of annual food production. The first group consists of those festivals such as May Day, originally associated with the spring equinox, as well as autumn festivals which include bonfires or the lighting of candles as an antidote to the dwindling of the sun's power.

Leicester Morrismen at Bradgate Park
1st May 1989
(Leicester Mercury)

The festivals of the farming year may be sub-divided into those which owe their origin to arable farming techniques, such as ploughing, seed sowing and germination or the harvest. The second group derive from the events of the animal husbandman's year, the birth of new stock, such as the lambing season, or the slaughter of animals.

The tensions associated with the uncertainty of the coming agricultural year found expression in festivals such as Plough Monday, with its rituals which are designed to ensure fertility following cultivation. The relief of a harvest safely gathered in finds its obvious outlet in ceremonies of thanksgiving. Intermediate between these is a festival of "first fruits", which marks the birth of the first lambs, or the harvesting of the first grains with thanksgiving rituals, but also looks forward to further bountiful produce to come.

It would not have been surprising to discover that people who inhabit the more northerly European latitudes should have taken a keen interest in the moment that the sun started to move northwards again, the winter solstice, with the consequent lengthening of the day. This is the moment that tells that spring is perhaps not too far away, and promises an end to long, cold, dark nights.

The Germanic and Scandinavian peoples of northern Europe, however, celebrated their principal winter festival, known as Yule, in November (on or about the 11th or 12th). The climate of northern Europe is such that few cattle could be fed during the winter, hay for winter feed being a restricted and valuable resource. This necessitated that animals above the number that could be kept over winter were slaughtered in November when the grass ran out, which then became a time of feasting, as well as a celebration of the harvest and the end of the agricultural year.

Associated with this festival was the bringing of greenery into the home. At a time when most trees had lost their leaves, it is easy to see that plants that remained green throughout the winter could be construed as having special properties, that enabled them to somehow defy death. Bonfires and candles, associated with light, also had great significance at a time of the year which was becoming ever colder and darker.

Once the celebration of the Nativity of Jesus had been fixed in December, the influence of the Christian Roman world on Northern Europe caused the Yule festival to move from November to December and combine with the Nativity celebrations. The resultant mix of symbols and ceremony is now seen as the "traditional" Christmas. An explanation of how this occurred, and further discussion of Christmas forms the subject of Chapter 5.

The fact that so many of us now live in an urban environment has failed to quell the lightheartedness and uplifting of the spirits brought by spring. The excitement of rebirth and rejuvenation is universal. This is the time of year when new crops appear above the soil. Consider the anxiety which our ancestors must have felt as they waited for those first few green shoots which heralded, and hopefully promised, food and security for another year.

This association with fertility naturally extended into relationships as well. An example is the Hindu spring festival of Holi, a festival of love and courtship. Part of the festivities traditionally associated with Holi is the throwing of grains or coconut into a bonfire as an encouragement to fertility, whilst in some parts of India Holi is marked by the singing of bawdy songs. Holi falls on the day of the full moon in the month of Fagun. In Leicester this falls sometime in the period March to April.

Two main themes are associated with the festival, perhaps indicative of its origins in the amalgamation of two previously distinct occasions. The festival is firstly associated with stories of the killing of the demon king Hiranya Kashipa by Vishnu. Embellishments to the tale concern the demon goddess Holika, sister of Hiranya Kashipa, who was connected to the Firegod, Agni. Her nephew, Prahlad, the demon king's son, was a devotee of Vishnu.

The demon king, unsuccessful in his attempts to turn his son away from good towards the path of evil enlists the help of Holika, who attempts to burn Prahlad to death. Holika, hence the name Holi, perished in her own flames through the intervention of Vishnu. The fire motif is still part of the festival's celebrations today.

The second theme concerns Vishnu, who comes to Earth as a baby, Krishna. Grown into a handsome young man, Krishna plays a prank on some cowgirls he finds bathing in a pool, and whose clothes he hides. He entices them out one by one in order to ask Krishna for the return of their clothes. All desire to dance with Krishna, but using his powers he deludes each into thinking they have danced with him alone, whilst in reality they are all dancing together in a circle. The story also tells that Krishna causes the cow-herd girls, or gopis, to throw coloured water at each other. Although these are the main stories associated with Holi, in different parts of India the details may vary.

One of the activities at Holi is the roasting of grains and coconut in a bonfire, before eating

Holi celebrations at Spinney Hill Park (Vasant Kalyani)

them as Prasada, or holy food. This probably points to origins as a spring equinox agricultural fertility festival. The theme of bonfires at this time, celebrating the victory of the Sun over the powers of darkness, often characterised as the victory of good over evil is a common one. A variation is the throwing of money or coconuts into a stream, to symbolise the throwing away of ill-luck, and its replacement by good fortune. This is still carried out in Leicester, as one of Leicester's Hindu residents explains,

"...when you have Holi, we throw money as a good wish, and an end of bad - evil, and we throw money, and some people throw coconuts and money into the water stream... in Spinney Hill Park there is a little stream, and the next day you go down, you see lots of money on the floor and coconuts rolling down the stream!"

Bonfires are often an adjunct of spring festivals celebrating the "return" of the sun and anticipating a bountiful harvest. In Gujarat, the ancestral home of many of the Leicester Hindu community, the direction the flames take is held to indicate the most fertile soil of the coming season, whilst babies and young children are carried around the fire in a ritual designed to protect them from harm.

This may be compared with the old Celtic spring festival of Beltane which also featured bonfires. Cattle were driven through the fires to protect them from disease, whilst women and girls would jump through the flames in order to secure a husband or to protect themselves at the time of childbirth.

The most remarkable feature of Holi is that it marks a time for the suspension of the normal social rules. The festival used to include elements of inter-caste rivalry, and of male-female role reversal, with women administering mock beatings to the men. One of the major customs at the festival of Holi is the throwing of paints and coloured dyes over one and other, in commemoration of Krishna and the gopis, and this can still be an important element of the festival, with old clothes being worn to minimise the damage!

Children use the occasion to blackmail their elders with threats of dye throwing if they are not given money! Leicester's Hindus who can recall celebrating the festival in East Africa or India remember it as a far more boisterous festival there than here. Worries that clothes might be spoilt or people may be offended by paint thrown over them cause the celebrations in Leicester to be inhibited. Holi is also marked in Leicester with a bonfire celebration in Cossington Street recreation ground.

Free style Kabbadi during the Sikh Festival of Hola Mohalla (Guru Nanak Gurdwara)

As a Sikh alternative to the Hindu festival of Holi, Guru Gobind Singh decided to hold a festival at the same time at Anandpur. The name he gave to this festival was Hola Mohalla. Probably the best translation into English would be "manoeuvres". The grandfather of Guru Gobind Singh, Guru Hargobind had been responsible for the foundation of a Sikh standing army. Guru Gobind Singh used the festival as a gathering together and training session for this army. Archery and wrestling contests culminated in a mock battle, the high spot of the festival, although there were also music and poetry competitions.

By the 1970s, May Day had virtually disappeared from the calendar of English Festivals, but in the past it was one of the most popular festivals of the year. Many of us may remember dancing round Maypoles as a child at school, innocent of the nature of the festival we celebrated, or of the fight, sometimes violent, to end it.

May Day has a pre-Christian origin, but was never assimilated by the Christian church in the way that Yule was. Its origins lie in the mists of early Roman history, in what was then part of the Greek Empire. Around 200 BC a cult worshipping the Phrygian (now part of Turkey) goddess of fertility, Kybele, was established in Rome. Celebrations included an image of the goddess being paraded through the streets in a carriage drawn by lions, with cymbals clashing and the eunuch priests dancing themselves into a such a frenzy that they cut their own limbs.

Frowned upon by the government, the festival dwindled in importance until resuscitated by the Emperor Augustus in 22 BC. Over the next fifty years the festival again grew in importance, with special emphasis being given to those aspects of the festivities relating to fertility. Integral to the celebrations was a procession to Kybeles' wood outside Rome in order to cut down a pine tree.

This, shorn of all but its upper branches in order to emphasise its obvious symbolism, was brought back into Rome. Here it was set up, decorated with flowers and other trimmings, and used as the centre piece for dancing and debauchery. The date for the commencement of these scenes of abandon, which went on for several days, was significantly March 22nd, the time of the Spring Equinox.

The expansion of the Roman Empire meant that festivals like this were introduced to countries such as Britain under Roman rule. Certainly the celebrations took root and flourished here. The transference to the first day of May is almost certainly due to this being the date of the Celtic festival of Beltane, which heralded the coming of summer. The Mayday festivities withstood all the efforts of the Christian Church to suppress them. Here is a description of the Mayday celebrations in England in 1583, over a thousand years after the end of Roman rule:

"For what clipping, what culling, what kissing and bussing, what smouching and slabbering one of another, is not practised every where at these dancings? All which, whether they blow up Venus' coal or not, who is so blind they seeth not. Against May, all the young men and maides, old men and wives, run gadding over night to the woods, groves, hils, and mountains, where they spend all the night in pleasant pastimes; and in the morning they return, bringing with them birch and branches of trees, to deck their assemblies withall. And no marvel, for there is a great Lord present amongst them, as superintendent and Lord over their pastimes and sportes, namely, Satan, prince of hell. But the chiefest jewel they bring from thence is their Maypole, which they bring home with great veneration, as thus. They have twenty or forty yoke of oxen, every Oxe having a sweet nose-gay of flowers placed on the tip of his hornes, and these oxen draw home this May-pole (this stinking Idol, rather) which is

covered all over with flowers and herbs, bound round about with strings from the top to the bottome, and sometimes painted with variable colours, with two or three hundred men, women and children following it with great devotion. And thus being reared up, with handkercheefs and flags hovering on the top, they straw the ground rounde about, binde green boughes about it, and arbours hard by it; and then they fall to dance about it, like as the heathen people did at the dedication of the Idols, whereof this is the perfect pattern, or rather the thing itself. I have heard it credibly reported (and that viva voce) by men of great gravity and reputation, that of fortie, threescore, or a hundred maides going to the wood over night, there have scarcely been a third of them returned home againe undefiled."
(some spelling has been modernised for ease of reading).

Puritanism was an extreme form of English Protestantism, which sought to purge the Church of England of ceremony, and particularly those ceremonies which echoed the ceremony of the Catholic Church. It rose to become a major factor in English social life during the latter half of the sixteenth century and the first half of the seventeenth century. The power of the Puritan ethic reached its zenith due to the identification of Puritanism with the victorious Parliamentarians in the English Civil War. Puritans assumed you could change belief and behaviour by legislation.

Not only did the Puritans rail against what they saw as the excesses of other Christian Churches, but they also condemned occasions of what were seen as riotous and unsavoury behaviour by the general population. The censorious quotation above is just such an example. In 1644, under the Commonwealth, the Puritans were finally successful in their campaign against Mayday, when along with Christmas it was abolished. The campaign to promulgate their morality was pursued fervently at a local level as well.

Even earlier than this in Leicester on June 1st, 1599, we find Richard Woodshawe a shoemaker, being accused before the Mayor and the Magistrates of speaking in favour of the May Day festivities, after the Mayor had caused the Maypole to be taken down. Woodshawe compounded his "offence" by re-erecting the offending pole. The fact that Morris Dancers, a popular entertainment abominated by the Puritans, were also present at the celebrations, caused further problems. This attempt by the authorities, no doubt mindful of the Puritan persuasion of the powerful local Hastings family, to stop the Mayday celebrations in Leicester had, within four years, brought the town to a state of riot.

In a May 1603 letter, from the Mayor, Mr James Ellice, to the Earl of Huntingdon, Lord Lieutenant of the County, the Mayor states that timber has been stolen from the (Hastings) family's woods near the town, in order to set up Maypoles within the town. Henry Hastings, Earl of Huntingdon, was a zealous Puritan, who encouraged a multitude of Puritan preachers to visit the town, all entertained at the corporation's expense.

On the 1st of May, which in 1603 fell on the Sabbath, the authorities tried to suppress the traditional Mayday celebrations, which included once again Morris Dancers. The letter, no doubt with an eye to absolving the Mayor himself of any blame for negligence continued,

"Now so it was, may it please your good lordship, the stewards notwithstanding, there was the same night many maypoles by an unruly band and a confused multitude of base people set up in the street, and the stewards' watch too weak to suppress the outrage."

There then followed a description of how the people were carrying on,

"with a most tumultuous uproar and outcry until Sir William Skipworth (a county gentleman)

came in, and dealing somewhat roughly, and laying hold of one Wood, a butcher, a most disorderly lewd person, brought him to me, whom I presently committed. Proclamation of departure was made to the rude audience, which was then contemned (scorned), and seconded the next day with `morrices,' and a great number of idle, rude company, many of them armed with shot, following them, morning and evening, the whole town throughout".

This resulted in a riot, with bands of the common people marauding around the streets, some of them armed with guns, although there is no record of firearms being used against the authorities. The town remained in a very disturbed state for the next two weeks, no doubt inflamed by the prosecutions brought against those whom the Mayor and his cohorts saw as the ringleaders.

The organisers of these Mayday celebrations had no doubt taken heart from the replacement of Queen Elizabeth, who had acted against such unruly behaviour, by her successor James I, who was well known to be a supporter of popular pastimes, and published "The Book of Sports" as an encouragement to their continuance. A Leicester Puritan preacher, Nathaniel Sampson, Master of Wyggeston's Hospital certainly saw the end of Elizabeth's reign as a setback for the Puritan cause. Following her death in March 1603, he preached a Mayday sermon in St Martin's, now Leicester Cathedral, bemoaning, in his view, the end of 44 golden years.

The Puritan triumph however was short lived. The restoration of the monarchy under Charles II in 1660 saw the return of the Mayday celebrations. Samuel Pepys, in Kent at the time, noted in his diary on May 1st 1660, that the people of Deal had put up two or three Maypoles with flags on them. The original meanings of Mayday were gradually lost however, and the festival dwindled in importance.

That it continued to be observed in rural villages though is borne out by a report in the Derby Mercury in May 1772. A rumpus was caused by some youths from Loughborough removing the Maypole from Quorn village at the dead of night. From the turn of this century onwards, a movement gathered strength to revive English folk customs. The May celebrations, shorn of their more dubious delights were deemed to be suitable for children. Here is a nonagenarian resident of Leicester reminiscing about May days some 80 years ago,

"May Day everybody had a pretty clean frock on and a pinny, you know those frilly pinnies that we wore, and a team who would have had to practice at it did the weaving round the Maypole on a piece of ground somewhere. Everybody couldn't obviously, only certain people could do it, and you went and watched it... we didn't do anything special on May Day except that it was a day's holiday from school."

Here is another memory from before the First World War,

"I went to school when I was five, I went to Mantle Road School which is off Empire Road off the Fosse... I can remember actually the place in the school where I sat... I remember the Maypole, where boys and girls used to dance round, we did what we called the "plait", and this "plait" was done to music, you see, the teacher used to play the piano."

and Maypole dancing continues to this day to be performed by children at school and village fetes.

The Morris Men too went into decline during the 19th century, only to be revived from the 1920s, and Morris dancing has continued to grow in popularity ever since. Once again the Morris Men of Leicester dance in Bradgate Park at dawn on May 1st, their mission in the words of the Leicester Mercury,

"...to encourage the sun to shine and the crops to grow..."

Belton Maypole dance 1963
(Leicester Mercury)

They perhaps might cast their minds back to a May morning at Bradgate House some 400 years ago. Here is a description of a May Day morn by Lady Mary Keyes, sister of Lady Jane Grey, writing in her "tablette book" (diary),

"Then, when the merrie May-Pole and all the painted Morris-dancers with Tabor and Pipe, began their spritely anticks on our beautiful green lawn, afore that we idle little Bodies had left our warm Beds would good Mistress Bridget, the Tire-woman whom our Lady Mother always commanded to do our Biddings, come and tell us of the merrie men a-dancing on the Green."
(some spelling modernised for ease of reading)

In line with the European tradition of celebrating 1st May as International Labour Day, in 1976 the government made May Day a public holiday.

For as long as humans have been farmers, the harvest has been an important punctuation mark in the year. Harvest festivals of some sort are a universal feature of all agricultural communities.

In Leicester, we are used to celebrating the harvest in the autumn, but we should remember that for peoples originally from warmer climes, harvest festivals may fall at different times of the year.

Baisakhi, of significance to both Sikhs and Hindus, was originally a first fruits festival, one of the traditional rites being to throw a few grains of barley into the fire as an offering for a successful harvest. Even in Leicestershire, barley is harvested much earlier than wheat, usually from around mid-July onwards. In the Punjab in northern India which enjoys a much warmer climate than the East Midlands of England, the barley is ready to harvest much earlier, around the middle of April, hence the date for the Baisakhi festival. The full significance of Baisakhi for Sikhs is discussed in Chapter 2, Fresh Starts.

The medieval Christmas was a longer holiday than even the one enjoyed in Leicester now. In the rural area around Leicester, work did not resume in the fields until the day after Twelfth Night, also known as the feast of Epiphany. The major task at this time was ploughing. The first Monday after Epiphany was known as Plough Monday. It was especially common in Leicestershire and other eastern counties for a ceremony of blessing to be carried out on the ploughs to be used for the coming cultivations. The ploughs were decorated and carried around the villages by young men, known as Plough Bullocks. Accompanying the ploughs were groups of male dancers, who performed a variety of Morris Dancing known as Molly Dancing.

This practice came to an end in Leicestershire around 1850. It was a time when many such old rural customs fell into disuse. Some traditions however take a lot of killing. In 1987, a group from Hinckley revived the old custom. Calling themselves the Hinckley Bullockers, they performed the traditional dances in several of the local villages.

Leicester, centre of a large rural hinterland, continued to play an important role as an agricultural market town even into the present century. The Harvest Home festivities were probably the most important seasonal festivities of the year as far as agricultural communities were concerned, and many farm labourers in the 18th century would not work for a master "who failed to provide them with supper and song in the hour of achievement". Also associated with Harvest Home festivities' pagan roots were corn "babies" hanging from the roof - figures made out of a sheaf of corn and dressed in human clothes.

The decline of Harvest Home was probably linked with the growth of industry and the movement of population from rural areas into towns. As agriculture became a more commercial operation, the paternalistic relationship between men and masters, based on mutual dependency, was also weakened. Harvest celebrations returned in a more sanitised form in the 19th century, as the Harvest Festival.

Though it is unlikely that many children now in Leicester help with the harvest, schools still mark the occasion. At many schools for instance, the occasion is celebrated by all the children bringing fruit or other food to school. The whole school meets together for assembly, to which local elderly people are invited, who later receive gifts of the fruit.

For Leicester's Polish community in their present urban surroundings it is difficult to celebrate the Harvest festival in the traditional manner. Back in Poland, the agricultural workers and their families would join the procession to the manor house, accompanied by the music of fiddlers. Heading the procession would be young girls in traditional costume, each bearing a wreath made from the produce of the harvest, a sheaf of twisted rye and wheat, intertwined with poppy blooms. Attached to this would be fruits from the orchards, plums, pears and apples, tied to the wreath with ribbons in gay colours. When the procession arrived at the manor house, the owner would greet all the guests with bread and honey served on a wooden platter. All dined together at long wooden tables. This was an occasion when all gave thanks for the successful harvest with singing and dancing.

This of course gives some idea of how Harvest Home was celebrated here in the past. Here is how the Leicester Polish community celebrate nowadays:

"We celebrate in Leicester as a thank you for the year that's gone. For all the work that's been done in the parish, by the people, for the people, with the people. And of course the dance troupe, this is when they have their first

Harvest Festival at St. Mary's Church, Knighton 1968 (Leicester Mercury)

54

showing of the dance they do for that year, it culminates in that... We have bread made in the shape of a sheaf of wheat, and we cut that up on the Sunday, because we do a repeat performance for the parishioners that couldn't make it to the dance on the Saturday night. We cut the bread up and give it to the parishioners as a token gesture of the harvest, of everything that culminated through the year, and you share it with everybody."

The Jewish festival of Passover was described in the previous chapter. Associated with the feast of Passover is Pentecost, which occurs 50 days after the first day of Passover. This festival is also known as Shavot, or the festival of Weeks. Pentecost celebrated the gift to the Jews of the five books of Moses, which include the ten commandments.

For Jews attending the synagogue at Pentecost there will be readings from the Old Testament, Exodus ch. 20, describing how the

Members of the Polesie Dance Troupe celebrating Harvest Festival (Polesie Dance Troupe)

commandments were given. Cheesecake and other dairy products are eaten at this time. The origins of the festival, however lie in a thanksgiving for the wheat harvest. Indeed it was originally known as the Festival of the Harvest, or the Day of the First Ripe Fruits.

Another Jewish festival associated with the harvest is the feast of Sukkot, also known as the Festival of Tabernacles or Booths. Once again there is a mixture of symbols and origins. The festival is celebrated from the fifteenth to the twenty second day of Tishri (October/November). The timing suggests that it may well have been connected with the grape harvest, and the production of wine, at the time of the autumn equinox, as well as an encouragement for the start of the autumn rains.

One of the principal elements of the festival today, however is the erection of a sukkah (usually translated as "booth", it is a temporary dwelling constructed of branches and foliage) outside the home. The sukkah both symbolises and commemorates the temporary dwellings the Israelites were forced to live in during their wanderings in the desert following the flight from Egypt. It is a tradition for Jews that one should live in the sukkah for a week in order to relive and share the experiences with the Israelites of the Exodus.

In order to make this as realistic an experience as possible, the sukkah has to be built in such a way as to leave chinks in the roof through which the stars may be glimpsed. Inside fruits are suspended from the ceiling, whilst the walls are decorated with children's drawings. Regrettably, the Leicester weather does not encourage this observance, but nevertheless, members of the Leicester Jewish community do still build sukkahs on their patios!

Immediately following the Festival of Sukkot is a day set aside for the final part of a cycle of readings from the Torah. A part of the Five books

of Moses is read every Sabbath during the year, the readings being completed on this day known as Simhat Torah. It is important, however, that as the cycle comes to an end, it is immediately started again with a reading from Genesis, so that the cycle is never completed, the Torah has no end. At the synagogue, the Torah, in the form of hand written scrolls, will be taken from the Ark and paraded around the synagogue. In Leicester, as elsewhere, there will be dancing and singing in the synagogue, and a festive meal to follow in the Community Centre.

Mealtime in the Sukkah
(Mrs S. Hood)

Hanukkah, or the Festival of lights falls in December. It commemorates events in Palestine at a time of Greek influence in 168 BC, when a Greco-Syrian leader, Antiochus Epiphanes defiled the temple in Jerusalem by the erection within it of idols, particularly to Zeus. A Jewish uprising led by Judah Maccabee (the story is told in Maccabees, chapter 4), was eventually successful in re-establishing Jewish independence. The day chosen for the re-dedication of the temple, following victory in 161 BC was the same day as had earlier been the time of its defilement by Antiochus.

It is likely however that its alternative name, and the ritual lighting of candles, signifies that the festival was originally connected with the winter solstice. The festival lasts for a period of eight days, a commemoration of the finding in the temple when it returned to Jewish hands of a small quantity of oil, enough to supply a candle for one day, but which nevertheless lasted for eight.

The tradition now is to light a candle on each of the branches of an eight branched candelabra for each of the days of Hanukkah, which last from the twenty fifth day of Kislev to the second day of Tevet. A single candle is lit the first day, two the second day and so on. Of course generally, outside Israel, Jews are unable to enjoy the same public rejoicing, but in Leicester, a candelabra, or menorah is set up in Victoria Park, so that all can share in this festival.

It is traditional also to enjoy the light from a candelabra at home. Here in Leicester, the candelabra is usually placed in the window, whereas in Israel, the candelabra are set up outside the houses. Associated with the festival are special foods, traditionally some cooked with oil such as potato pancakes ("latkes") and doughnuts.

Menorah on Victoria Park 1993
(Leicester City Council)

Two seasonal festivals have virtually disappeared from the Leicester calendar. The festival celebrating the first fruits of the wheat harvest was known as Lammas, and was traditionally celebrated on the first Sunday in August. The name derived from the Anglo-Saxon word "hláfmaesse" meaning loaf mass, the loaves of bread from the first of the wheat harvest being consecrated in the church.

The Christian spring fertility festival is Rogationtide. Once again it has fallen into disuse, the decline starting during the last century. Held in the fifth week after Easter, the parish priest, followed by the inhabitants of the parish, set off to walk, or perambulate, around the parish in order to mark the boundaries. The priest carried a cross, whilst the parishioners bore peeled wands of willow, sometimes decorated with a small bunch of flowers. Unusually, the Rogationtide procession from St. Mary's in Leicester was held only once every three years.

Ancient parish boundaries ran from landmark to landmark, a bridge, a stile or an ancient tree, often known as the "Gospel Oak". At each of these landmarks the procession halted whilst the priest recited a litany or rogation calling for fertility and a bountiful harvest. The festival was introduced into England early in the eighth century and had a convoluted history. Originating at Vienne in France in 470 AD, the ceremony had been extended to the whole of France following the Council of Orleans in 511 AD.

Other processional ceremonies had been instituted in Rome by Pope Gregory around 598 AD as a Christian alternative to the ancient Robigalia, an early Roman fertility festival featuring processions. The exact story is unclear, but the various processional ceremonies eventually developed into the medieval Rogationtide processions.

It is a tribute to the longevity of cultural customs, that any seasonal or agricultural festivals are still held at all. The seasons of the agricultural year have very little relevance to an urban population which is used to buying its food supplies at the local supermarket. Of course, most seasonal festivals have now been incorporated or merged into religious festivals. All the more incredible therefore that Mayday has resisted all attempts to abolish it down the years.

SOCIAL DRAMA

Festivals are a key factor in a community's definition of itself. Apart from their religious meaning, may also be thought of as social drama. Drama, because as in a play, a planned sequence of staged events takes place, gradually building to a climax. Social because this is a drama in which all can take part, every citizen has a role to play at Diwali or Christmas, even if it is just to go and look at the lights. The same at Eid purely by wishing Muslim colleagues at work Eid Mubarak. All of us realise the collective potency of being able to say "I was there, I did that, I took part".

Caribbean Carnival
(Leicester City Council)

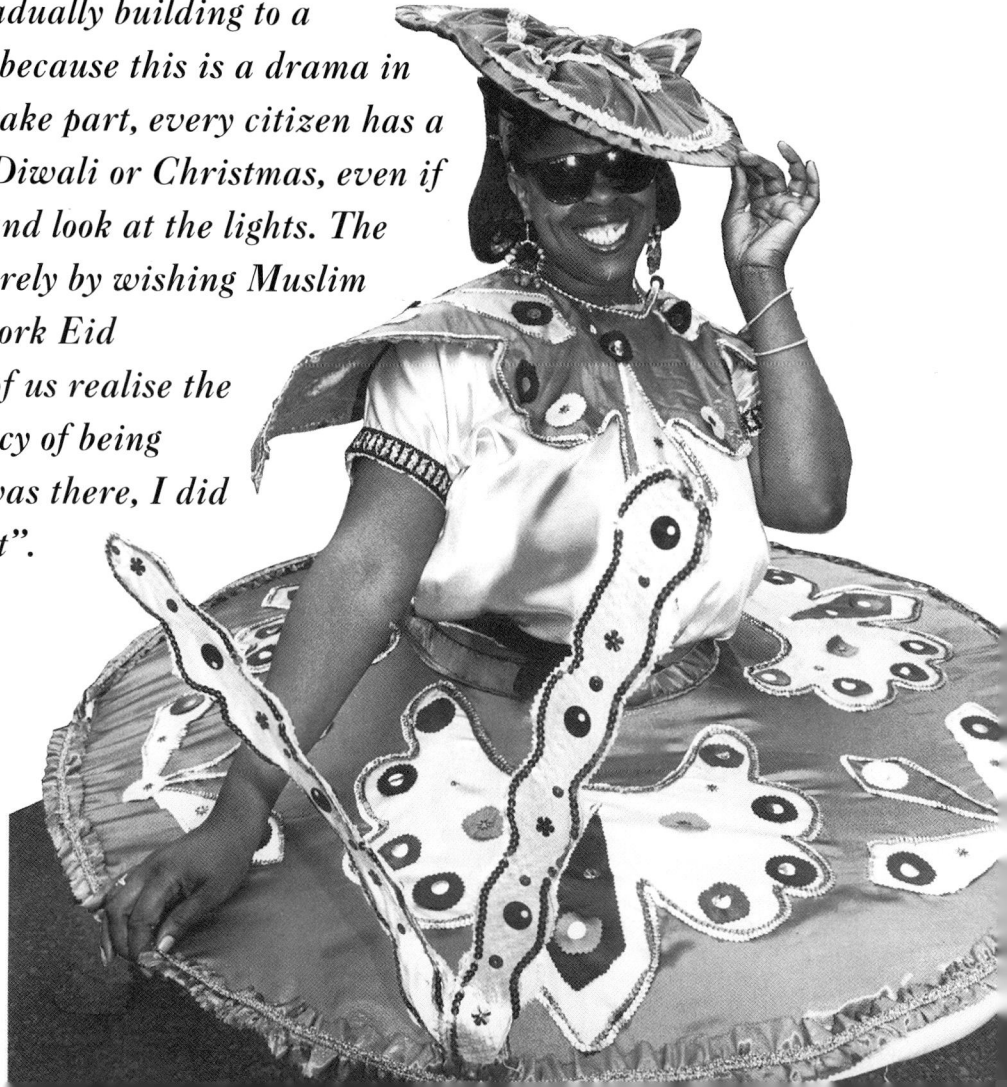

Social also because the drama defines the roles of the participants. It is an opportunity for displays of status and power. An opportunity to display the cohesiveness and solidarity of a community grouping. Festivals are a time for the mayor to don the robes of office and affirm the power of the local government. Recognition of this need for public display of power may be seen in the provisions of an Act of 1555,

"all and every person that shall be elect and chosen to execute the offyce of the mayoralty within the said towne of Leycester at every principall feast and other tyme accostomyd shall wear for the honor of the king and queen's majesties... and for the worshippe of the said towne scarlet, as of ancient tyme yet hath been accustomed."

(some spelling modernised for ease of reading)

In point of fact the mayor wore his scarlet robes at Christmas, New Year, Twelfth day (after Christmas, observed as Epiphany, the final day of the Christmas celebrations), Easter, Whitsuntide, and on fair days. This Act was obviously re-affirming a practice which had been customary for some considerable time.

Whilst festivals may have similar explanations for their origins, individual communities develop different ways of celebrating the event. The Greek Orthodox Church for instance displays many changes of emphasis and ritual in which festivals are celebrated compared to the western Churches. Over a period of time this can lead to a particular festival, or a way of celebrating a festival, becoming completely identified with one cultural or ethnic group. The festival, and its way of celebration can become a matter of great pride for the group concerned.

A major institution of medieval urban life in a city such as Leicester was the religious gild. The medieval gild fulfilled several functions within the community. In some ways it was almost like a friendly society. Payments made to the gild on a regular basis ensured that a member and his family would be taken care of in times of ill-health. The gild's main business however was not with life but with death. Craft gilds started in a similar way, but also represented the commercial interests of their members.

The medieval residents of Leicester, as elsewhere in England, were obsessed with the fate of their immortal souls. Worried that their souls might be subject to the torments of purgatory to the end of time, they paid their dues, or made their endowments to the gilds.

The gild took care of their souls by building chapels, often as adjuncts to existing churches, known as chantries. Here, priests would say obituaries and light candles for the souls of the dead. The prayers for the departed were performed on the anniversary of the person's death, possibly more often. The execution of this service became a lucrative role for many priests, who often came to live in some luxury. Resentment towards the clergy articulated by reformers such as Wycliffe, known originally as Lollards, dates from this time, around the end of the fourteenth century.

The Chantries were dissolved by an Act of 1545, one of the final pieces of legislation of Henry VIII, although most were not put down until further legislation by Edward VI in 1547. Their collective wealth proved too great a temptation for central Government, which pocketed the proceeds from the sale of their assets.

It is perhaps of some significance that the date of the foundation of the Corpus Christi Gild in Leicester was 1349 or thereabouts. The Black Death, which ravaged the country around this time accounted for the death of between a quarter and a third of the population. The gilds were operating in a buoyant market place. Indeed, the gild was enlarged in 1392 by William Humberston, when it maintained a total of four priests in St. Martin's, engaged in prayers for the

COGNIZANCE OF CORPUS CHRISTI GUILD.
(From Guild Roll, dated 1542.)

souls of its members.

In medieval Leicester, rival gilds competed for membership and for status within the community. One of these gilds, that of Corpus Christi (Body of Christ), still has a presence in the town today. Its meeting hall, now known once again as the Guildhall, became the Town Hall, where the burgesses of the old Town Corporation met.

The Gild of Corpus Christi became the major socio-religious institution in the town. Membership of the Gild of Corpus Christi was virtually obligatory for all who sought a leading role in the civil governance of the town. Indeed, the position of the Master of the Gild carried greater status

and influence than that of Mayor, and Masters of the Gild had invariably held the office of Mayor beforehand.

A rival gild, that of St George, the patron Saint of England is not so well remembered. The fraternity of St George also possessed their own Hall, which stood near the eastern end of St Martin's Churchyard. The Gild of St George was not involved with the town government, as was the Gild of Corpus Christi, or with parochial affairs in the same way as other gilds.

The Gilds of Corpus Christi and St George had a chapel each in the Church of St Martin, now Leicester Cathedral. In the chapel of St George, over the altar was a life-sized figure of the saint, clothed in steel armour, mounted on a richly caparisoned steed. The public face of the Gild was the annual procession. The Gild of Corpus Christi held two major public processions each year, one on the feast day, and one at Whitsuntide, when other gilds associated with other churches, most importantly that at St Mary de Castro, all made their way in solemn procession to St Margaret's Church.

St. Margaret's was the destination of these processions as it was associated with the Bishopric of Lincoln, the seat of diocesan government for the Leicester area. Featured in the Whit-Monday procession from St. Mary's were players representing the twelve apostles. Each one identified by the parchment placard he bore stating his name. As the procession was in honour of the Virgin Mary, an image, possibly a statue, of the Virgin was carried through the streets under a canopy born by four persons, preceded by musicians. Young girls, parish virgins, were also part of the procession.

Of course, rural churches also had their processions, and these traditions can persist over long periods of time. The following description of Whitsun in a rural village is remembered by a Leicester lady from the first quarter of this century,

The last re-enactment of the
Riding of the George, 1984
(Mr P. Bryan)

"Whitsuntide we used to start from the church, and we used to walk all round the village, it was a long walk, the Canon and his daughters used to join, everybody was in, all the scouts, all the guides, everybody. We used to stop at the war memorial and hold a service there on the village green, and then we used to go down into the next village and hold another service there and then back to the church, just to finish the service. You were supposed, and it was nice if you did, to get a new dress, but we didn't often get a new dress I'm afraid. That was the day we were supposed to be dressed up, and we used to call it 'walking round'."

The major public display of the Gild of St George was held some time between the Saint's feast Day, April 23rd, and Whitsun. The festival was known as the Riding of the George. These public processions by the Gilds were without doubt the major festival occasions of medieval Leicester. The expense of mounting the Riding of the George became so great that as the fortunes of the gild declined the Corporation was forced to contribute to the expenses.

For instance in 1498, we find the Corporation deciding that all the members, depending on rank, should contribute to the pageant either 4d or 6d, or hopefully, "more if they please". We also find regulations that the Master of the Gild could be fined by the Corporation if the Riding was not carried out, whilst the mayor and chamberlains could be fined, with proceeds to the Gild, if they did not enforce the Riding of the George.

Little in the way of contemporary eye witness accounts of the Riding of the George ceremony in Leicester has survived, although an item from the Corporation accounts for 1536, which records a payment of four shillings for the "dressing of the dragon" at least suggests that probably what transpired was a major procession through the town, with a mock battle between a mounted St George, wearing the armour from the chapel, and a dragon, probably similar to the mock dragons used at the Chinese New Year festival. Certainly this is confirmed by surviving descriptions of similar events in other towns.

Members of the local nobility attended and were entertained by the Mayor and corporation. Judging by the surviving accounts of expenditure for wine, the entertainment was on a lavish scale. The more lowly inhabitants of Leicester were not only expected to attend the event, but their attendance was enforced by local laws. We have a record of one such ordinance from the year 1466, which states that commoners who did not attend the Riding of the George would be fined six pence.

The procession through the town, starting from the gild's hall in Town Hall Lane, then known as Holy Rood Lane, culminated in a special Mass in St Martin's, where the gild's chapel was located. Hanging behind the altar in the gild's chapel was "a paynted clothe", almost certainly a painted representation of St. George slaying the dragon. Following the service, the assembled worthies retired to the Gild's hall for the food and wine, and the transactions of the gild's business.

The Riding of the George came to an end with the reformation. In the Churchwarden's accounts for St Martin's in the year 1547, we find the rather sad entries recording the sale of the "horse that the George rode on" for one shilling as well as other items from St George's Chapel. The re-introduction of Catholicism by Queen Mary, between 1553 and 1558 saw the brief resumption of the annual event, judging by the record of a payment for "sent George harnes" which occurred in 1554.

The actual St George in question is a little obscure. Supposedly a Christian officer in the Roman army at the time of Diocletian, who was put to death during the purges of Christians carried out by that Emperor, his feats are said to include the deliverance of a heathen city, and its

Queen, Margaret, from the attentions of a local dragon. In gratitude the citizens are said to have embraced the Christian faith. The figure of "The Margaret" figured in the medieval processions

His espousal by the English as their national Saint is due to his alleged appearance on at least two occasions to lend a hand to the crusaders in the Holy Land, the most notable appearance being at the battle of Antioch in 1098/99, when the besieged crusaders broke out of the city. English (actually predominately Norman) crusaders brought the story back with them to this country. His day, supposedly the date of his martyrdom was declared a Feast day in 1222.

Quite why George was singled out and honoured in this fashion is difficult to discover. St Demetrious and St Mercury were also supposedly seen at the battle, whilst the lance which pierced Jesus' side at the Crucifixion was purportedly discovered in the city during the siege, and was tied to a banner at the head of the troops as they marched out of the city to confront the Turks. The crusaders were near to starvation at the time, a condition which facilitates hallucination.

Of course St George's day continues to be celebrated. A parade of Scouts and Cubs marches through the city to a service at St Martin's, and the flag of St George flies over public buildings. For many people, however, the significance of the day has been forgotten. From time to time some other activity marks the day, such as in 1993, when pupils from Judgemeadow Community College, dressed in traditional costume gave a display of maypole dancing and stick dancing in Market Square. The College headmaster, in his capacity as Market Crier presided over the occasion.

Whilst St George is the patron Saint of the English, and is associated with English national identity, the Welsh, Irish and Scots also have their particular National Days associated with feast days of their patron Saints, St David, St Patrick, and St Andrew. Here is one of Leicester's leading Irish residents talking about St Patrick's day, and its meaning for him, and Irishmen everywhere,

"...ironically, when I was young in Ireland, it was the one day when all the licensed premises were closed. I think there were only two days of the year, which were St Patrick's Day and Christmas Day. One of the funny things about it was that although they were all closed legally, they were all open illegally! That was part of the fun of the thing for the people. There used to be a lot of parades, floats, that sort of thing. The pipe band would march and the Scouts Brass Band..."

For the Irish, there is a certain ambivalence to the celebrations, as it is both their National Day and a religious festival. This tension is heightened by the fact that Ireland is a predominately Catholic country, where fasting for Lent enjoys a much greater significance than it does for the non-Catholic residents of Leicester. Here is how the Irish have attempted to resolve this conflict

"...when I was young, Lent, which is the six weeks before Easter, was observed fairly strictly, and a lot of people for religious reasons used to abstain from food etc. very similar to the Muslim practice at the moment at Ramadan.

In my youth it was just as strict within the Catholic religion. St Patrick's Day always fell in the middle of Lent, it still does, I mean, from the way it falls, no matter where you've got Lent, St Patrick's Day comes somewhere in Lent, and St Patrick's Day was always regarded as a day when Lent was suspended for a day. So it usually amounted to a big feast or a good party etc, and everybody used to religiously resume Lent the following day. St Patrick Day was a day out!"

It is important for Leicester's Irish community that St Patrick's Day continues to be celebrated,

"...in Leicester, in the morning at St Patrick's Church on Beaumont Leys Lane there's usually a Mass, traditionally attended by the Lord Mayor of the City, followed by a reception afterwards.

There's an all day celebration going on at St Patrick's club on Abbey Street. There's music there right from the Church service in the morning. There's music on all day after that. There's one band on in the afternoon and another one on at night. It's wall to wall people! Because that's so crowded there are many other smaller events throughout the city, mainly in church halls...."

Leicester has a small but cohesive Irish community, mainly the result of immigration here towards the end of the last century, but swelled by the numbers who arrived in the 1950s. Keeping their cultural heritage alive is very important,

"...I find that my culture, the Irish culture is as different as anything I have come across from other cultures. Certainly it is something worth preserving, and it is why I am so pleased when I see the younger generation coming along who take an interest in it."

The Scots too have their national day. In fact the Scots really have two. St Andrew's day falls on November 30th, whilst Robbie Burns, the poet who encapsulates all things Scottish is remembered on Burns Night on January 25th. Scots emigrated from their homeland in large numbers during the last century.

Scots engineers made a major contribution to the building and operation of the railways on the Indian sub-continent, and it may well have been the presence of two major railways in Leicester that brought Scotsmen here. Whatever the reason, by 1900 there was a thriving Caledonian Society in Leicester. In 1908, we find the Leicester Daily Post carrying the following report on the St Andrew's Day banquet. Organised by the Caledonian Society, and held at the Grand Hotel, around sixty people attended,

"Before the dinner Piper Insch, arrayed in spick and span National costume, blew the shrilling bagpipes, and later on when the company were

assembled around the festive board, ushered in the steaming dish of haggis - that seductive product of culinary art - to the rousing strains of `The Cock o'the North'.

Councillor J.McCall, President of the Society - Alderman Thos. Smith also present - gave a toast to the Society, remembering that the object of the association was to keep alive the patriotic feelings which were characteristic of Scotsmen, and to afford them an opportunity of expressing Scottish sentiments, hallowed memories, historic incidents, and above all for the fraternisation - in spirit - with kindred societies at home and abroad."

The report continued with a description of Scots and their characteristics,

"a race of cool, keen, thrifty businessmen, clever administrators, great colonisers and strong governors".

Whilst festivals may be a means of expressing social dominance, they may also become a way that a minority group maintains its self esteem and cohesion. A statement of cultural identity and pride in one's ethnic group.

The Welsh too have their National Day. It falls on March 1st, and commemorates the death of St David on that day in 588 AD. St David was the head of the Celtic church. As the Anglo Saxons spread throughout England, pushing northwards and westwards, the Celts, the original British still carrying the vestiges of Roman civilisation, were marginalised in Wales and Cornwall.

The adoption by the Anglo-Saxons of the Roman Catholicism brought by St Augustine and described elsewhere in this book, led to

Members of the Leicester branch of Comhaltas Ceoltoire Eireann (Stuart Hollis)

attempts, finally successful, to bring the Celtic church under the control of Rome. The Welsh people however continued to resist English rule. It was not until around 1283-84 AD that organised resistance to English rule was finally overcome by Edward I.

Whilst the English may have ruled, Welsh culture, despite determined efforts on the part of the English to destroy it, refused to die, and enjoyed a revival during the 19th century. Many Welsh people have left Wales to seek work in England. Many have sought work in education, and the Welsh are well represented in Leicester's schools. Leicester's Welsh community have a thriving organisation, the Welsh Society. It meets regularly at Vaughan College, and celebrates the Welsh National Day, St David's Day, by holding a special dinner and drinking a toast to their patron Saint.

People from the Caribbean Islands started arriving in Leicester from the early 1950s onwards. The problems encountered by people of African-Caribbean origin who have settled in Leicester are quite unique. The settlers who came to Leicester from the Indian sub-continent, whether Sikh, Hindu or Muslim brought with them a quite distinct way of life and set of values based on hundreds, even thousands of years of cultural history.

For the Sikhs for instance, it was a relatively simple matter to hire a hall for a day, take some carpets for sitting on, and lo, there was a Gurdwara. Not perfect but it served as a community focus. A social nucleus which could raise funds towards acquiring a building to give material embodiment to cultural institutions. The first Gurdwaras, such as in New Walk, were acquired in this fashion in the late 1960s.

For the African-Caribbean settlers, things were different. The importance of festivals as an integral part of the structure of a culture has already been discussed. The cultural roots of African-Caribbeans had been left in West Africa when their ancestors were forcibly shipped across the Atlantic to provide the human muscle that was the foundation of the wealth of the West Indian sugar plantation owners. There can be little doubt that traditional festivals were lost in the process.

Around three thousand years have elapsed since the Jews escaped from slavery in Egypt, but the reverberations of their exultations of freedom are still celebrated today at the Passover Festival. That this is seen to this day as fundamental to Jewish culture gives some indication of the enormity of the cultural vandalism of the slave trade.

Although freed from slavery, the original culture of the African-Caribbeans had been totally destroyed. In its place had been imposed such facets of English culture as it was deemed necessary for their exploitation as a cheap labour force.

In many ways the education imparted in the Caribbean had an English orientation. Indeed, many of the early immigrants had served in the British armed forces during the Second World War. The hostility and rejection encountered by the immigrants when they arrived in England gave rise to shocked bewilderment.

The Sikhs from the Punjab, the Hindus from Gujarat or the Muslims from Sylhet never expected when they arrived to be part of English culture, the African-Caribbeans did. Rejected for the most part by the host community, forced to develop their own cultural framework, it should be no surprise that one of the first signs of an emerging African-Caribbean self-awareness and identity was a festival. A festival what is more that looked back to African roots for its inspiration.

Back in the Caribbean, Carnival, whilst taking some of its inspiration from the Mardi Gras parades of Shrove Tuesday was from the start infused with memories of the African homeland

and culture. In Trinidad, even by 1847, Carnival had developed the form we know today. Mass processions, multi- coloured pageantry and mocking of those in authority. The themes and symbolism of that pageantry though hark back to Africa.

Slavery and its associated brutalities did not come to an abrupt end. The trade in humans for slavery by British ships and businessmen was ended by an Act of Parliament in 1807. Some thirty years however was to pass before the slaves in the sugar plantations were emancipated. The plantation owners received millions of pounds of Government money to compensate them. At the time it was considered an act of kindness that this was not paid as a loan to be recovered from the slaves themselves, who received nothing.

The traditional date of celebration of the end of slavery is August 1st, Emancipation Day. The actual day was a Monday, and in Antigua, for instance, Carnival always takes place on the first Monday in August, although there is some variation, with Trinidad celebrating Carnival in February. Leicester Carnival takes place on the first Saturday in August.

One of the first major concentrations of African-Caribbean settlement was in Notting Hill, an area of North Kensington in London. It was here that Carnival was reborn in England. The date chosen was the August Bank Holiday, then held at the beginning of August and not the end as now. The growth of the Notting Hill Carnival continued throughout the 1970s, despite opposition from local groups. In 1986, more than a million participants were estimated to have attended the Notting Hill Carnival in that year.

The Notting Hill Carnival is now the largest street festival in Europe and its success inevitably encouraged other African-Caribbean communities, such as Leicester's to form their own Carnival committees and reproduce their own local Carnival.

Leicester's African-Caribbean Carnival dates from 1985, and one of its founders, Elvy Martin has been quoted as saying that she was keen to see Carnival started in Leicester for the sake of the children,

"There was nothing in Leicester for African-Caribbean children. I wanted them to see they had a culture which was beautiful. We wanted to see their culture portrayed as good".

Here is another of Leicester's African-Caribbean community, Bernard Francis, an enthusiastic organiser of the Carnival talking about the importance of Carnival and children,

"So, when Leicester Carnival started, the first year I actually dressed up my kids in clown suits. I have still got the clown suits here now, they're actually right in the office here now, and got them dressed up because you know that my childhood was coming back, and I wanted to relive my childhood in my children, so I had my three boys dressed up as clowns. They took part and me and my wife actually got involved and were selling things in the Park and things like that."

Dressing as clowns is one of the traditional themes of Carnival. This quote emphasises once again the way that festivals provide a focus for the community, and are the point where the culture is handed on to the next generation. A central theme to Carnival is that everyone should take part, giving solidarity and cohesiveness to the community.

Of course here things are not the same as they are in the Caribbean. Here is the same person talking about the differences between his home in Antigua, and Carnival in Leicester,

"There is one thing I am not happy about in Leicester. The firms and the wider community don't seem to get involved and sponsor Carnival like they do in the Caribbean. In the Caribbean all the firms get involved at some stage by actually sponsoring people and troupes to actually get involved and make things, give materials and you

*Caribbean Carnival
(Leicester City
Council)*

know, really get involved. I find it difficult why the community at large don't get involved. Because, it's as if it's just the Caribbean thing, so it's nothing to do with us, we'll just come and look on. But that is not what Carnival is all about, or not from what I can recall. In the Caribbean you cannot find a wider variety of people, because you know, everybody who owns businesses, or the majority of people who own businesses are white people, or foreigners, people from Asia and places like that. They sponsor things."

Some degree of bewilderment is understandable. The Leicester Carnival attracts between thirty and forty thousand spectators, one would have thought that was a big enough captive audience to have made it worthwhile for local firms to be interested in sponsorship. In the Caribbean, the Carnival organiser is often a public employee, responsible for approaching local firms for sponsorship.

As ever with festivals, even if one is not taking part as a performer, it is a time for dressing up in the best clothes possible. Here is Bernard Francis remembering how it used to be,

"Obviously you put on your best gear. In the Caribbean, I mean, clothes is something that for everybody is like a competition how you dress, I mean, you dress nicely. For Carnival you put on your new frock, if you like, if you're a woman, and a man a new shirt and pants, colourful or whatever. So even though you are not taking part in the procession you would be a picture to look at because you've got your new sneakers on or whatever it might be at the time."

In the Caribbean islands, Carnival is a pivotal point of the year. As soon as one Carnival is past, plans are being laid for the next. There is the same period of build up over the weeks before the main event as at Diwali or Christmas. Knock out competitions, for instance, to see who will be in the finals on Carnival Day itself. There are teenage pageants, and schools also generate excitement

before the big day itself by incorporating Carnival oriented activities into the curriculum.

Carnival of course also calls for special food. In England memories of the Caribbean homeland can be conjured up by the smells of baked snapper! The fish which form the basis of this Caribbean dish can be bought in Leicester fish market. Traditionally the snappers are baked with a stuffing of garlic, onion, bacon, mushrooms and bread crumbs. Encompassing and dominating all the activities of Carnival though are two themes. Themes which are fundamental and pivotal to African-Caribbean culture, freedom and belonging. Here is how Bernard Francis summed it up,

"Carnival IS involvement, Carnival is ONE thing... comes Carnival, everybody, the rich, the poor, the down and out, the sick get involved. I mean, even the dead get involved, if you like, they come alive! Carnival in the Caribbean is everybody, who never speak to somebody in a hundred years, will speak to them on that day because it is Carnival. Who cares. WE ARE FREE, WE ARE PEOPLE AGAIN"

Navratri and Dussehra fall in the Western calendar in the months of September or October. In the Hindu lunar calendar, Navratri, the name means nine nights, is celebrated during the "bright" half of the month of Ashvina, i.e. the half of the month when the moon is waxing, from the time of the new moon. Dussehra, literally 'the tenth' is the following day, although in some areas of India it also describes the whole ten day festival. In Britain the festival falls in the period of September/October.

The main theme of the festival is a feminine one. On one level, worship would be given to the great Goddess, Devi, in the guise of Durga who slew the buffalo demon Mahishasura, indeed another name for the festival is Durga Puja. Many small villages throughout India, however, would also worship their own local Goddess during the

*Navratri celebrations at Granby Halls
(Leicester City Council)*

festival. On the tenth day, the victory of Rama over the demon king Ravana is also celebrated. Apart from Durga, another Goddess to be celebrated at Navratri is Saraswati, the Goddess of learning, the arts and beauty. In Gujarat, an important part of the festival is the dancing performed by the women and girls. These are traditional dances such as the dandia raas (stick dance) and the garba.

Originally in India, this festival, whilst celebrated by all, was much promoted by the ruling aristocracy, who were responsible for mounting extravagant and colourful pageants. Changes in the political structure mean that this element is now disappearing from the celebrations.

A very special way in which one can take part in a religious festival is by undertaking a pilgrimage. The major religious pilgrimage which takes place in the world today is the Islamic Hajj, the pilgrimage to Mecca. One of the "Five Pillars of Islam", every Muslim is expected to make the pilgrimage at least once in his or her lifetime. The Hajj takes place during the 12th month, Dhul-Hijjah, of the Islamic calendar.

Several ceremonies are enacted during the pilgrim's time in Mecca. Two of these are the circumambulation seven times of the Ka'aba, and walking between the hills of al-Safa and al-Marwa. The Ka'aba is believed by Muslims to have been built by Abraham when he visited Mecca, and is thus the oldest building in the world devoted to the worship of the one true God.

The two most important acts of the Hajj are to attend the service on Mount Arafat, on the ninth day of Dhul-Hijjah and the Festival of Sacrifice, or Eid-ul-Adha. The service at Mount Arafat is the essential act of the pilgrimage. The pilgrims leave Mecca before sunrise for the journey to the Mount, which stands in a large enough plain to hold all the two million or so pilgrims who congregate at Mecca each year. Amongst these will be some from Leicester's Muslim community. Here is one of those pilgrims from Leicester talking about his pilgrimage and what it meant to him personally,

"I have made four visits to Mecca and am very lucky in that respect. The visit for Hajj was about eight years ago. I went in the company of about thirty people from the Islamic Centre (in Leicester). It was a fantastic experience and the journey of a lifetime as they call it, and certainly was the journey of a lifetime. Over in Mecca you see millions of people from different parts of the world, joining in the same activity which is performing the Hajj. It is difficult to describe that because that has to be experienced, but I spent over three weeks there and enjoyed visiting

30ft tall effigy of Ravana – the Demon King
(Leicester Mercury)

71

Mecca and Medina and performing all the Hajj rituals. I came back with very rich memories of the whole journey, and made lots of friends as well.

For me it was a most fantastic experience because most people, somehow, go there when they are old. For a long time I had the ambition to go there as a young person, which fortunately I did, because there's a lot of physical activity. You have to run from one place to another. There's a lot of walking to do, there's a lot of travelling to do, and old people often suffer a lot while doing that. As a young person I found it very, very enjoyable to be able to cope with all that journey. And of course it is something which according to the Faith gives you like a new birth. After you have been for Hajj you are almost like as if you have been born again, and what you do after that, what you do after the Hajj, you have to watch, because it is a new opportunity to make your behaviour better, and your dealings with other people better than they have been before."

The Pilgrimage culminates on the tenth day of Dhul-Hijjah with Eid-ul-Adha. It is also known as Eid-ul-Nahr, the Festival of Immolation, or Eid-ul-Kabeer, the Great Festival (as it lasts one day longer than the Festival of Breaking the Fast), Eid-ul-Fitr, as well as Qurbani Eid, the Festival of Offering. For those Muslims who have undertaken the Hajj, the Festival is celebrated at the village of Mina, on the way back from Mount Arafat to Mecca. But for Muslims the world over the Festival is also celebrated at home in their own communities.

The Festival recalls the willingness of Abraham to sacrifice his son Ishmael to God. A feature of the festival everywhere is the sacrifice of a goat or lamb, in remembrance of the act of Abraham in sacrificing a ram to God in thankfulness, when God spared the life of his son Ishmael. The place where this drama took place is Mina, and the exact spot is marked by the great Mosque of Mina.

In many parts of the world, the sacrifice would be carried out at home, whilst of course for pilgrims who are on the Hajj, the sacrifice is made at Mina. For Leicester's Muslim community, the sacrifice is carried out under supervision at an approved abattoir.

All of the festivals described in this chapter are dramas on a national or even international stage. They enable the participants to feel part of a much wider community, and re-enforce the cultural bonds between communities which are widely scattered. In the final chapter consideration will be given to some dramas played out on a smaller stage.

CHRISTMAS

Christmas is the major festival in the Leicester calendar. The word 'traditional' is so much associated with Christmas that it is taken for granted that Christmas in Leicester has always been celebrated in the same fashion. Nothing could be further from the truth. Indeed during one period of English history, the Commonwealth under Oliver Cromwell between 1650 and 1660, Christmas was actually abolished by the government. Many people at the time though were extremely unhappy about the loss of what they saw as their rightful festivities and holiday.

The impact of Christmas is now so great as to seriously distort the pattern of the year. The length of the Christmas holiday, which was two to three days in the 1950s, now stretches to around a fortnight. Many Leicester businesses are totally dependent on their Christmas trade to sustain them throughout the rest of the year

What might be thought to be the most central and unchanging feature of Christmas is the date which marks the birth of Jesus, December 25th. Even this however has been subject to change, and indeed certain Christian denominations to this day celebrate Christmas on another date. So how and when did Christmas start to be celebrated?

When the early church came to consider the anniversary of the birth of Jesus, there were immediate problems. None of the gospels in the Bible which record the life of Jesus give any clear idea of the year of his birth, let alone the actual date. Until the fourth century AD no mention is made of any celebration to mark the birth, or nativity, of Jesus. The first record we have of Christmas

being celebrated on December 25th is in a Roman calendar of 336 AD.

Prior to the celebration of Christmas, the eastern half of the Roman Empire, centred on Constantinople, celebrated the feast of Epiphany, to mark the baptism of Jesus, on January 6th. From around 350 AD, the Christian church in Syria added the commemoration of the Nativity to the Epiphany celebrations, still on the 6th January.

Possibly the first official pronouncement regarding the date of Christmas was by Pope Liberius in 353 AD, who set the date of Christmas as December 25th, although leaving the feast of Epiphany on January 6th. Quite why this was done is not clear. It may be significant, however that there were two important festivals in the Roman calendar at this time. These were the Saturnalia, and the Natalis Solis Invicta, a festival of the cult of Mithras. The Mithraic celebration was a winter solstice festival marking the rebirth of the sun. The likelihood is that Pope Liberius was looking to provide Christian alternatives to these two pagan festivals.

The coincidence of the date of Christmas and the winter solstice caused a certain amount of dissent in the early church. The identification of Jesus as the "light of the world", at a time of ceremonies marking the victory of light over darkness as the days started to lengthen again, brought accusations of the celebration of Christmas being nothing more than sun-worship.

The Syrian and Armenian churches continued to celebrate Christmas on January 6th, which was the actual date of the winter solstice in the Julian calendar. It is of interest to note that this was the date in Alexandria of the celebration of the birth of Osiris, a God of the ancient Egyptians, which was celebrated at the winter solstice. There is some evidence to suggest that the confusion over the two dates, December 25th and January 6th, is due to confusion between the Alexandrian (Egyptian) calendar and the Roman calendar over the exact date of the winter solstice.

The celebration of Christmas is surrounded by a bewildering array of symbols - trees, mistletoe, fairies, candles, paper chains, seasonal foods etc. Of these symbols we now associate with Christmas, none is so important as the Christmas tree. Whilst there is now a proliferation of various plastic and tinsel imitations, the significance of a tree brought into the house originally lay in the beliefs surrounding the apparent death defying ability of evergreens. This of course was an adjunct of the winter solstice celebrations in northern Europe associated with the rebirth of the sun. In warmer climates evergreens have never had this significance as the difference between the seasons is much less marked.

The Christmas tree is a relatively recent custom in this country, and its introduction from Germany, where the practice of setting up a tree in the house at Christmas was common, is usually credited to Prince Albert, the husband of Queen Victoria, in 1841. However the German Christmas tree had been publicised here before then. The poet Coleridge had spent Christmas in Germany in 1798, and published an account of the setting up of a decorated and candle-lit tree in the house where he was staying. He also described the custom of the children putting presents under the tree for their parents.

The Christmas tree started making an appearance in a few English households, usually due to the presence of a German guest or employee, from around 1820 onwards. In 1840, it was reported in Manchester, where a number of Germans had settled, that the habit of bringing the tops of pine trees into the house at Christmas was spreading rapidly amongst the local population. Undoubtedly the popularity of the tree received a boost from the publicity surrounding its presence in the Royal household.

A stable and secure family was an institution much admired by Victorian society. The royal family, although Prince Albert did not exactly draw universal admiration, was seen to embody all the virtues of family life. A lithograph published in 1848, shows the Royal Family at Christmas all grouped around a Christmas tree. The tree is over six feet in height and stands on a table. At the bottom are displayed the presents for the children, dolls, a railway engine, soldiers on horseback. The branches of the tree are decorated with sweets and paper toys. The branches all hold candles, and the tree is topped with an angel. The whole scene is a model for what is now seen as a traditional Christmas.

The Christmas tree rapidly gained acceptance in Leicester as elsewhere. In 1841, the Leicester Journal carried an article describing how Christmas was celebrated overseas and mentions the German "tree of gifts and bon-bons". By 1858, the practice of bringing a tree into the house was well established in Leicester. In that year we find a Leicester retailer, Hunters of 34 Gallowtree Gate, advertising that "articles suitable for dressing the Christmas tree" were available for sale costing from one penny upwards.

Whilst the tree itself was a novelty, the giving of presents or the bringing of greenery into the home was not. The pine tree merely supplanted a much older English custom of bringing evergreens indoors, whilst the giving of presents at Christmas, particularly to children was long established.

Fewer and fewer households now hang a sprig of mistletoe at Christmas, yet the mistletoe represents a far older tradition than the Christmas tree, and is a vestige of a much larger decoration known as a "kissing bough" or "kissing bunch". The "kissing bough", consisted of a crown-shaped wreath of evergreen, bearing a ring of candles above it, which were lit on Christmas Eve, Christmas Day and thereafter until Twelfth Night. From around the edge hung apples, the whole framing the most important element, the sprig of mistletoe.

Why should this decoration have been replaced by the tree? Mistletoe had long been frowned upon by the Anglican church, who, quite rightly, saw in it whispers from a non- Christian past. But there is something deeper at work here. Society today tends to look to the past for models of how life should be. The Victorians were excited, self-confident and enthusiastic about the future. Novelty, improvement and change were central to the Victorian world. The Christmas tree was viewed as a progressive innovation.

Traditions such as this do not just suddenly stop, but gradually fade away. Here is how an octogenarian from Leicester remembers apples being hung up for fun and games on Christmas Eve during her childhood in the early years of this century,

"Mother's favourite! Grab apple! She always saved an apple with a stalk on and tied it up on top of the door frame and you had to stand with your hands behind your back and bite this apple. It was getting the first bite, once somebody had got the first bite you were alright, but it was getting that first bite, it used to go all round your chin, and all round your face!"

Holly, of course, shares the same evergreen properties as mistletoe, and was also used to decorate houses. All Christmas decorations such as paper chains, holly wreaths, etc. derive from these evergreen decorations. The choice of trees by the Germans, and smaller shrubs by the British, is purely the result of biological accident.

Britain has only two indigenous evergreen trees, the Scots Pine, rare in lowland England, and the yew. The yew, whilst widespread, was planted mainly in churchyards and was thus unsuitable. Mistletoe, which grows as a parasite on oak trees was far more common. The extensive adoption of the Christmas tree as a symbol of Christmas was only possible from around the mid-nineteenth century onwards due to the large scale planting of

Christmas cards c1920
(Leicester City Council)

commercial evergreen softwoods. The Christmas tree, with its association with family values, and given a seal of approval by the royal family, was seen as a novelty to be promoted as an antithesis to the old custom of kissing under the mistletoe. It is ironic that a well established British pre-Christian custom should have been supplanted, in the name of progress, with a Germanic custom which had grown from the same basic beliefs and practices.

The "Yule-log", another long established Christmas symbol, now tends to find expression as a decorated chocolate cake, but at one time was an actual log. Customs have varied over time, but usually a log was placed on the hearth, often decorated with greenery. On Christmas Eve it was lit using remnants of the previous year's log as kindling. The log was kept alight all during Christmas Day. Ashes from the log were sprinkled on the ground outside to promote fertility, and a small portion saved for the following year. Apart from providing fertility for the new crops, the log was also thought to provide light and warmth for the souls of the dead.

Christmas cards now form one of the most significant features of the Christmas season. These are also a relatively modern addition to the Christmas scene. From around 1830, the custom grew of sending a

Christmas, New Year or birthday letter to friends and acquaintances, with a small poem as a heading. In 1846 the first example of a genuine Christmas card appeared, with an artist's drawing on the front.

The first commercial Christmas cards date from around the 1860s. As the century progressed the cards became more and more elaborate. Leicester certainly took up the fashion for Christmas cards as early as anywhere else in Britain. In 1858, Hewitt and Moore of 15 Granby Street were advertising Christmas and New Year's Notepaper, Complimentary Cards and Verse Cards.

The way that Christmas has been celebrated has changed dramatically over the centuries. Until the time of the Reformation, England was a Catholic country. The celebration of Christmas was not however seriously affected until the triumph of the Puritans during the English Civil War. In 1644, the Puritans had decreed that Christmas should be observed as a 'fast day' only, and made further attempts to suppress all popular revelries, even to the point of using troops to confiscate meat being cooked on Christmas morning. Whilst the abolition of Christmas was heartily disliked by many, its re- introduction following the Restoration of the monarchy in the shape of Charles II in 1660 did not see Christmas regain its former medieval and Catholic glory.

For instance on Christmas Day in 1663, the diarist Samuel Pepys, whilst noting that he had a pleasant dinner at home still went to his office to work during the evening. By the early 1800s, although Christmas was celebrated on a private level, on a public level it had almost withered away. In 1828, for instance, the Leicester Journal never bothered to mention Christmas at all, and even in 1840, when it published on Christmas Day itself, the only mention of Christmas concerned a luckless lad named Raven who had absconded over the Workhouse wall, only to be recaptured and in the words of the paper "denied his Christmas treat".

From the early 1840s onwards the pace of change gathered momentum until by the turn of the century, the Christmas we know today was well established. The utilisation of Christmas to market consumer goods, whether or not they had any seasonal significance whatsoever was well established. With the commercial rise of Christmas came the lengthening of the holiday towards the present week or so, although in 1890 a correspondent in the Leicester Mercury was bewailing the fact that Leicester was lagging

Advertisement in a Royal Opera House programme 1885 (Leicester City Council)

behind the rest of the country by not declaring a four day holiday at Christmas.

For manufacturers and retailers, Christmas offers three main "marketing opportunities". The purchase of presents for others, the purchase of food and drink in excess, both for self-consumption and for entertainment, and the purchase of goods for the home, often to impress visiting friends and relations. There is no doubt that the exchange of presents is a powerful way of establishing and binding relationships.

Present giving is a major feature of festivals in many cultures. A very important element is the giving of presents to children. This is a common theme for instance at Diwali, Eid, or the Chinese and Vietnamese New Year. Whilst presents were no doubt exchanged within the family from medieval times, it was the spread of newspapers, and particularly of advertising which saw the development of the orgy of present giving of today.

From the 1850s in Leicester, local retailers were starting to advertise certain articles as suitable as gifts, mainly to start with, as gifts for children. In 1853, the problem of what to buy one's daughter for Christmas was addressed by one local shopkeeper who suggested that the collected "POEMS OF FELICIA HEMANS" would solve some of the difficulties with which many fathers were no doubt deeply troubled in the following words,

"Here is a volume in which high poetry and deep passion are united with feminine delicacy and unsullied moral purity. Here is a volume a father may give to his daughter on her birthday, or on some day of this gift giving season, with a feeling not less confiding or holy than that with which he gives his child her night and morning blessing or Kiss."
(Leicester Journal, Dec 16th 1853).

In 1858, S.Catlow of 76 Humberstone Gate was advertising a range of children's books

suitable as Christmas gifts, including many on natural history, birds, plants etc., as well as others of a rather more morally uplifting nature. By the turn of the century, rather more familiar items featured, when F. Herington of 16 - 20 High Street were offering dolls that talked and slept, whilst for boys there were models of Gatling guns (a type of machine gun), marines and men of war.

One of the more noticeable retailers was Heringtons, whose advertising campaign had got under way in November 1858 with an announcement of the opening of their Grand Christmas Bazaar offering English and Continental novelties. By December they were advertising themselves as the "electric lighted bazaar". This extension of the Christmas season backwards into November had begun in the last half of the nineteenth century.

In 1870, John D. Horn of 6 Carts Lane had declared open their Grand and Bewitching Christmas Continental Fancy Fair in mid November. Note the use of the word "Continental" to suggest flair and excitement, it was employed in much the same way that "high tech" is used now as a description of the very latest and up to the minute item.

Gifts for adults did not figure as an important item until the last quarter of the century. Once again it was the latest technology which featured. In 1878, H. Gee of 53 Market Place was drawing gentlemen's attention to the latest, silent, Willcox and Gibbs Sewing Machine, as an ideal present for their wives. Half a century later, in 1930, the electric gramophone was advanced, in an article in the Leicester Mercury, as being a gift that one's wife would be pleased to receive.

Christmas 1920 saw the start of special Christmas gifts for motorists. The gadget of the time was the brass holder for the vehicle excise duty disc, compulsory from January 1st 1921. Above all though, the most important feature of Christmas gifts is the excitement they engender amongst the children. This is how one Leicester resident remembers Christmas morning about seventy years ago,

"Well we thought it was a wonderful time, because it was the birth of Christ that was the most important wasn't it? And then of course we looked forward to hanging our stockings up. Mind you we didn't get very much in them. It would probably be an apple and an orange, a sugar mouse and a new penny and perhaps a few nuts, that was about all... stockings were hung on the bedrail. We opened them Christmas morning, in the dark, we'd nudge one and other and say 'he's been'! We never had any lights upstairs, only candles."

In a child's mind, presents at Christmas are associated with Father Christmas. He too has a long history, probably originating with the Norse god Woden, the bringer of gifts, who drove his reindeer through the long dark nights of the northern winter. Christianised by the church, probably around the fourth century he became identified with Nicholas, Bishop of Myra. Known as Saint Nicholas, he became the patron saint of children, and his feast day was 6th of December.

Christmas over the centuries proved a magnet which has now captured the celebrations of his day, celebrations which saw children, a few days beforehand, leaving notes on the window sill or a ledge in the chimney, telling him of the toys they

Father Christmas in Town Hall Square
(Leicester City Council)

wanted. On his special day, Saint Nicholas would return to distribute the gifts. The explanation of the stocking at the foot of the bed is rather more difficult to explain, although it was known as a custom in continental convents for nuns to hang stockings on the abbess' door asking for the protection of Saint Nicholas. The next morning when they returned the stockings would be filled with sweets.

In 1850 there was no hint of censure or shame in the raffle for Christmas week patrons of Leicester's Theatre Royal, who were automatically eligible for the draw to see who would win the two hampers of wine and spirits, one for the pit and one for the gallery. A few years after, the Eagle Brewery in Lower Charnwood Street was advertising its "Yule Ale, noted for its body". But at the same time Cook's Temperance Hotel in Granby Street was promoting a Christmas Temperance Festival at the New Hall.

Just after the First World War broke out in 1914, Leicester pubs were forced to shut at nine pm in order to guard against drunkenness on the part of the troops, who in any case had been denied any Christmas leave. At the same time the Church of England Temperance Fund was advertising in the Leicester Mercury for donations. The advertisement stated that intemperance was one of the major evils of the war. Doubtless the participants could think of many greater evils of war than excess drinking.

The temperance movement was a reaction

Alderman Amos Sherriff handing out free Christmas dinners at the old Workhouse in Swain Street, Leicester in 1922 (Leicester Mercury)

against the worst abuses of alcohol. Whether it had much effect on the population at large is questionable. Looking at the Christmastide Mercury around the early years of the century, it is very noticeable that there was a major increase in the number of advertisements for alcohol, although few, if any, of them made an explicit connection between alcohol and Christmas.

Another drug, nicotine, has also managed to forge a relationship with the Christmas festivities. In 1900, a Leicester tobacconist, James Smith, with branches in Eastgate and Cheapside, was drawing attention to the suitability of cigars as Christmas gifts. By the 1930s brands such as Craven 'A', in special Christmas boxes of 100, were being heavily promoted as ideal gifts.

Many festivals are seen as times to give charity to the poor. This theme for instance is central to the Muslim festival of Eid. Christmas is no exception. Victorian society was especially pious in this direction. It also presented a marvellous opportunity for the sanctimonious to pat themselves on the back for their generosity.

Whilst no doubt feeling especially virtuous during the year for keeping the costs of maintaining the Workhouse poor to an absolute minimum, the wealthy at Christmas could feel especially proud to see their names publicised as givers of charity. During the latter half of the nineteenth century it was common for the Mercury to print a list of the benefactors who had contributed to the provision of the workhouse Christmas dinner.

A Leicester Mercury reporter visited the Leicester Workhouse in 1890. He reported that the entrance bore a banner "Welcome to our Guardians". The Guardians were the management committee whose chief responsibility was maintaining a standard of living within the workhouse which would discourage any from seeking entrance. The principle followed was that whilst the Workhouse should provide a safety net to prevent actual starvation, any employment outside, no matter how mean the remuneration, or appalling the working conditions, would be preferable to seeking its dubious sanctuary.

The Mayor was in attendance at the Workhouse dinner that Christmas of 1890, although he did not partake of the Christmas fare on offer. He made a speech stating that he would enjoy his Christmas dinner all the more for seeing them eat theirs. Little doubt about that, but one suspects that the inmates did not care too much, anything would have been better than their normal monotonous food, provided by local suppliers who submitted the lowest tender. Although it must be said that the poor outside the Workhouse walls fared little better.

Many special dishes have become associated with Christmas. Turkey, plum pudding, mince pies, Christmas cake, all are described as traditional Christmas dishes. Until the development of fodder crops such as turnips during the seventeenth and eighteenth centuries, it had long been the practice to reduce drastically the number of beasts to be kept during the winter. This meant that at Christmas one either ate preserved, i.e. salted, cured or dried meat, or alternatively birds of one sort or another.

The spiced dishes associated with Christmas owe their origin to various ways of disguising the flavour of meat which was beyond its best. For the aristocracy and royalty, the bird associated with Christmas, until the turkey was introduced from Mexico around the 1540s, was the swan, with lesser mortals making do with goose.

Around the turn of the century in Leicester, beef was still a treat for Christmas, although there were one or additional bonuses from having a goose, as this story from around the eve of the first world war shows,

"We had beef, a very large piece, a haunch of beef on Christmas Day. We tried a goose one Christmas, but geese should never be eaten at

Christmas... have them at Christmas and they've put on their winter fat, and then they're very rich, and you've got a lot of goose grease. We used to use the goose grease, rubbed on your chest if you had a cold, oh yes! Just refine it, put it in to boiling water, and then let it set, then take it off and pot it up, jar it up. Then you had the goose grease on your chest, and some brown paper put on top of it, so that it didn't come through everywhere, and it kept the warmth in."

When it came to buying a bird for Christmas early this century, there were specialist shops, and keeping the bird until Christmas was a problem solved by the retailer in a traditional way as remembered here,

"...just round the corner from the Clocktower, not facing Gallowtree Gate but (East Gate) was Berry's the fishmonger. Now Berry's was THE fishmongers in Leicester, a very, very, powerful shop, a big shop with a huge frontage, and every kind of fish you could buy there, every kind of game, venison, the lot, you could get from Berry's. Come Christmas, all their orders for geese and turkeys and chickens and what have you, were all hung right the way up the building. The whole building was covered with birds of all varieties and all sorts until Christmas Eve, or round about Christmas Eve."

Christmas is above all a family festival. It is a time for children to return home, for relatives to spend time together. This is a writer in 1829, telling Leicester Journal readers about the family side of Christmas

"How delightful is the approach of Christmas to the schoolboy! He has long been absent from his paternal abode; he has been labouring we will suppose, vigorously and unceasingly; he has experienced, perhaps, the most rigid and unflexible feeling on the part of his preceptor; consequently the anticipation is inspiring, when he shall bid farewell, at least for a period to scholastic discipline, and severity - close the dry and difficult books over which he has so often pored - frequently with so little success - and visit again those tranquil scenes, where all the bliss of home is realised, and all a parent's fondness is poured forth....Christmas, too, is a period of deep interest, because it is the time of domestic and relative temporary re-union. How many members of families never see each other collectively assembled, except on Christmas day! Local situation - the ever recurring engagements of business - and a variety of circumstances which might be enumerated, prevent frequent meetings; hence the period of Christmas is a time fixed on, as an opportunity of enjoying domestic festivity, when the scattered members of families may meet beneath the same parental roof, and experience all the sweet interchanges of domestic and relative endearment. There is something peculiarly sacred and tranquillising to the spirit. The gratulations expressed - the affection indulged - the animation experienced - are delightful to witness - but when it is contemplated what fluctuations are realised - what bereavements are sustained - what sufferings are endured from one Christmas to another - a powerfully affecting impression is produced on the mind."

This association of Christmas with reunion means that separation at Christmas is even more poignant. Of course separation may be by choice, but in the memories of many Leicester people are recollections of the enforced separations of World War II. The war brought other privations. Food was very scarce and traditional Christmas dinners a fond memory. For those in the armed forces abroad, Christmas could be spent in unfamiliar surroundings. Here are Leicester people remembering their wartime Christmases,

"Can you remember we used to make (Christmas) trimmings out of the blueprints. We used to go down the drawing office and speak nicely to them and they used to let us have the old blueprints. We used to fold them in three and

Berry's shop on the
Sunday before
Christmas 1953
(Leicester Mercury)

hang them up and they used to look quite pretty. We used to trim the factory up, we used to have a happy time at Christmas. We used to make Christmas puddings but it used to be substitutes, I can't ever remember at Christmas that we didn't have a Christmas pudding, I suppose what they did they saved up the rations, and you'd have to go without something else. There weren't Christmas trees, I can remember one year in the war my dad went out and got a holly bush from somewhere, although I don't know where he got it from, and we had that trimmed up. We managed at Christmas somehow... I know after we'd been bombed out we went back into the house about October or November time, and we had sausages cooked on the fire for our Christmas dinner that first year."

The sausages were probably mainly breadcrumbs too! The ingredients for cakes could be somewhat unusual too,

"I've got Christmas recipes, I've got recipes we used for Christmas for 1940, you know, where you used semolina and a spot of vanilla essence, so that you could make marzipan, all that sort of thing. It was surprising the many things that you could do... how do you make them a cake, you can't make a cake with dried egg, it didn't work but it had to be done... so we set about it, my neighbour had got an egg and we'd got no fat. I know! We'll use liquid paraffin... and it came up all right. It looked lovely, but when we put it on the table we did have to tell the children, now, only one piece, if you have more than one piece you'll feel poorly. Lots of little things like that were done..."

Schools too, during this difficult time, did what they could to make Christmas as normal as possible for the children. This is a Leicester teacher describing a wartime primary school Christmas,

"We kept up Christmas... we always had a children's Christmas party, tiny little Christmas presents, a penny each for the tiny little ones you could get for the children, and we were rationed as to what we could give each other, we could spend two shillings for each of us. But the children had a party, very simple food, and we had our own party afterwards.

I can remember some ladies... they worked at Morleys, I think it was Morleys, they were some relation I think, that sold materials in town. They used to make little bags for the children of the off-cuts of the material. So at Christmas time there would be a bag for each little girl that they could keep their knitting or their sewing or their toys in, boys had one as well."

Occasionally, fate can intervene at Christmas in a quite spectacular fashion, here is the same teacher talking about a very special Christmas,

"Mr Greasely over the road, the baker, won something on the football pools, it wasn't Littlewoods then it was Moore's Football Pools, and he appeared in the School and said he wanted to know the number of children in the school, which was 146 then, and he appeared the next day with 146 cream buns, one for each child to celebrate."

One of the effects of war is that those serving overseas have to celebrate Christmas in unfamiliar surroundings. In this connection we are apt to think of the men who did the fighting, but many women served overseas during World War II. Here is how one lady from Leicester came to celebrate Christmas in Bombay,

"I volunteered for the WAAF (Women's Auxiliary Air Force) in November 1941. As I'd worked in a shoe shop they said, 'right, stores it is for you'... I sailed from Liverpool the beginning of December 1944, and it took a month to get to Bombay... I was in technical stores, sending spares to the front line... Christmas came, my first in the far east. We all managed to get a new dress made up for the Christmas dance. We had a lovely Christmas dinner, but it seemed funny *eating turkey and Christmas pud in the heat."*

Because of its nature as a punctuation mark in the year, other events tend to congregate in the period just before Christmas. In 1850 for instance, Leicester Collegiate School announced that it was splitting its examinations into two groups, some to be held in the summer, others to take place at Christmas time. History and Mathematics were the chosen subjects for the season of good cheer.

The results of these examinations were published in the Mercury in descending order of merit, causing no doubt a little less cheer in the less successful households. Of such public interest did these examination results become that two years later in 1860, the Mercury carried out an analysis more in the manner of the reporting of the Boxing Day race meeting at Kempton Park.

Many of the images we now associate with Christmas have their beginnings in the last century. How ironic then to find a writer in the Leicester Mercury of the 1880s bemoaning the passing of the "traditional" Christmas. Christmas past, living on in the memory, always seems to have been somehow more jolly. An editorial in the Leicester Mercury in 1920 summed it all up rather well,

"The ideal Christmas is the one we used to have. Those of us who are approaching the "sere and yellow" stage of life hark back to the days of our youth when "Christmas was really Christmas", full of jollity and innocent revelry, the memories of which have mellowed with the passing years, and are treasured accordingly. But curiously enough our grandfathers used to say the same thing, and we are rather driven to the conclusion that the typical Christmas symbolises a memory of a generation..."

Different Christian communities place different emphases on the celebration of Christmas. The Leicester Polish community for instance sees Christmas Eve, known as Wigilia, as the main focus of the Christmas celebrations. Christmas Eve is the time for exchanging presents, but the children only receive them after the first star has appeared in the sky. Some of the older Polish traditions of course have fallen into disuse.

Memories of older agricultural traditions were preserved in the placing of sheaves of corn in the room as a token for a good harvest the following year, whilst hay, now seen as a remembrance of the hay in the stable where traditionally Jesus was born, was placed beneath the table cloth, although this is probably a later explanation for an earlier pagan custom.

The traditional Christmas meal for the Polish community is also held on Christmas Eve. In common with all who celebrate Christmas this is a time for families to congregate and re-affirm their loyalties. There is a Polish custom to leave an empty chair at the table ready for an unexpected guest, or in remembrance of a family member lost through the year. The number of courses has to be an odd number, 7 or 9 for example, whilst for no course must there be an odd number of people at the table, as this signifies a death in the coming year.

The Christmas holiday now ends immediately after the New Year's Day bank holiday. The traditional time for the ending of the Christmas celebrations was Epiphany on January 6th. As we saw earlier, for the Eastern Church this was the festival commemorating the baptism of Christ, whilst in the western world it marks the manifestation of Christ to the Magi, the three wise men from the east. Epiphany marked the real end to the year. The next traditional festival was Plough Monday, and by then everybody's thoughts were firmly fixed on the new agricultural year.

For Catholics, such as Leicester's Polish community, whilst Christmas decorations have to be taken down by Twelfth Night or Epiphany, or ill luck is sure follow, the real end to the Christmas season is at Candlemas on February the 2nd. Instituted by Pope Gelasius in Rome in AD 494, probably as a Christian alternative to the Lupercalia, the festival originally marked the presentation of Christ at the Temple, as well as the Purification of the Virgin Mary. The festival took the shape of a procession with all the participants carrying candles, hence its later name of Candlemas. This almost certainly marks the incorporation of elements of earlier celebrations marking the rebirth of the year and spring fertility. The general celebration of Candlemas started to dwindle in England after the Protestant Reformation, when the concept of blessing the candles was seen as idolatrous.

For many children, and their parents, Christmas would not be Christmas without a visit to the Pantomime, and for many in Leicester this means a visit to the De Montfort Hall. These same children will have spent the weeks before Christmas earnestly rehearsing the school Christmas Nativity play or celebration. Widely different nowadays in their content and performance, the two share a common origin. In late medieval Leicester, it was commonplace for dramas to take place within the churches. The accounts for St Mary de Castro in 1491 contain an item for payment to "players" just after Christmas.

The use of churches for plays, at Easter and Whitsun as well as Christmas was largely discontinued, firstly due to the Reformation and secondly due to Puritan zeal. In 1581, we find the Corporation placing restrictions upon the performance of plays, although as these restrictions continued to be restated from time to time we may infer that it was not a popular move.

A survival continued in the villages around Lutterworth however, where the "Christmas Mummers Play" continued to be performed into the latter half of the last century. One of the most popular themes for the late medieval plays was the story of Robin Hood. We find this subject being used as the basis for an early Christmas Pantomime in Leicester in 1875. In that year the

Theatre Royal was advertising:

Mr Elliot Galer's
Third Grand Christmas Pantomime

HARLEQUIN ROBIN HOOD AND HIS MERRY LITTLE MEN, OR KING RICHARD AND JOLLY FRIAR TUCK

in which Mrs Elliot Galer will make her first appearance this season and sustain the character of Robin Hood.

The pantomime season does not now usually commence until after Christmas, but Mr Elliot Galer's offering got under way on December the 24th, and was advertised to be performed every day thereafter.

The use of the Church for performance also continued. In 1920 it was reported that St Marks Church was responsible for a Christmas tableau of presentations of scenes of the Annunciation, the Nativity, the visit of the shepherds etc. A stage was erected in the chancel, and children played the part of angels. How many proud parents have watched their less than word perfect offspring as angels in the School Nativity play?

It would be unthinkable to leave Christmas without a mention of the weather. It is impossible to think of Christmas without the accompanying imagery of stage coaches in a snow covered landscape, robins in the snow, the candlelight glow from a cottage window throwing pools of light on snow covered ground. The basis for so much of this imagery, of course, are the scenes depicted on Christmas cards.

Winter in
Town Hall Square
(Leicester City Council)

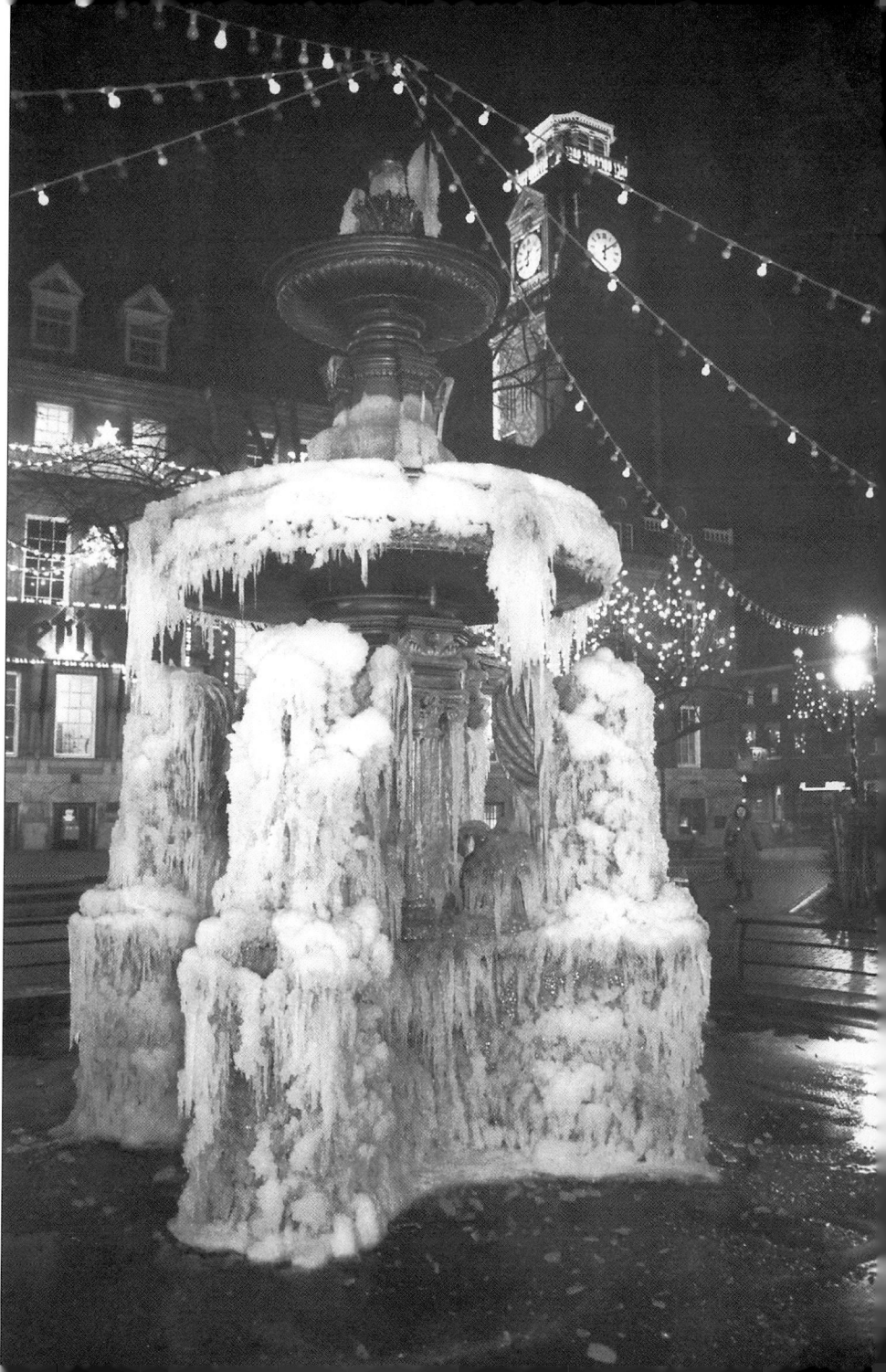

It is generally excepted that Charles Dickens was responsible for much of the popularisation of what we now see as traditional Christmas scenes. His descriptions of Christmas in novels such as A Christmas Carol, did much to fix the concept of a "white" Christmas in the popular imagination, although a helping hand along the way was provided by Bing Crosby.

During the latter half of the 19th century, warmer Christmas weather had become noticeable. In 1868, for instance, it was noted in the local press that,

"So far as the weather can have effected (sic) such a joyous period as this, the Xmas of 1868 has been unquestionably dull. For some considerable time before Xmas there had been an almost daily downfall of rain; the atmosphere had been damp, foggy and cold, but the clear, healthy bracing air which we are accustomed to associate with the annual visit of Old Father Christmas came not."

The following year, a correspondent in the Leicester Mercury offered an explanation for the lack of appropriate weather at Christmas, in an article entitled "Why Christmas weather is not so cold as formerly" readers were asked to consider another effect of those eleven missing days, removed from the calendar in 1752,

"The real reason of the change is, not that the old-fashioned weather has deserted Christmas, but that every Christmas since 1752 has deserted the old-fashioned weather. On that memorable change from the old style to the new, an alteration of eleven days took place in the seasons and immediately what had been the 5th of January in 1751 became the 25th of December 1752. Now if we recollect, it is just about that on the 5th of January and onward from it that the coldest weather of the year comes, even in these later days of ours. The great frost of nearly two years

back, the most intense that has occurred in England since scientific tests have been widely used, began on the 3rd of January, and the records of the average of years will show much the same result... "

In fact the weather now around Christmas tends to be chilly but settled, with wet weather and storms following shortly afterwards, but as ever with the English weather nothing can be taken for granted. Whatever the weather, the imagery of a "white Christmas" looks set to persist for a long time yet.

There is one fact which, in all the discussion of the trivia of Christmas, must not be ignored. For many of Leicester's citizens, Christmas denotes the foundation of their religion, and is marked by attendance at Christmas services at the city's many churches and places of worship. The Christmas message of "peace and goodwill to all" however is universal. Here are the words of a local Christian describing what Christmas means to him

"The celebration of Christmas for a Christian is recalling the birth of Jesus Christ. To a Christian, this event signifies God's new plan which started 2000 years ago. Before this event, from the time of creation, people had the choice to believe in God. Since then, with the birth of Jesus Christ (God in human form), people have had the opportunity to become reborn NOW and move into the experience of the disciples by a step of repentance, and asking Jesus Christ into their lives. God sent his only son into the world that people today may be in His kingdom before death. Because of this supreme sacrifice by God, Christians celebrate Christmas when God sent His only son to be a connecting link. The joy of Jesus' birth is therefore incredibly good news, showing God's love for all mankind."

HIGH DAYS AND HOLIDAYS

Not all festivals have momentous religious or cultural reasons for their existence. There are many festivals which may have a purely local reason for their observance. There are others, which although celebrated nation-wide, do not have the impact on everyday life of say Diwali, Eid, Baisakhi or Christmas. Mothers' Day and Valentine's Day for instance, whilst they might bring enjoyment to many members of the community do not bring about a total cessation of normal activity. In this final chapter we shall be looking at some of these occasions, both now and in the past.

Amongst the festivals of Leicester which have either been forgotten altogether or which have lost their meanings are several to do with the affirmation of privileges. Until 1628, to the west and north of Leicester there existed a great wedge of Royal Forest still commemorated in the names of Leicester Forest East and West. It extended in area to some 50 square miles, and included Enderby, Narborough, Lubbesthorpe, Braunstone, Glenfield, Kirby Muxloe, and Desford, as well as much that is now within the city boundary, such as New Parks and Western Park.

The distinguishing feature of a Royal Forest was not that it was an uninterrupted tract of woodland, but that the normal rights and privileges the local population may have hoped to enjoy were restricted by the Crown.

Valentine's Day card c1920 (Leicester City Council)

We now see woodland usually in terms of a resource for leisure. In medieval England, for the common man, woodland was a resource of a much more fundamental nature. It was a source of building materials, fuel, and food for animals. Within a Royal Forest, these rights were non-existent, or had to be paid for.

Hunting in the Royal Forest was an activity restricted to the King and his chosen followers. Over the course of time, the nobility also sought the right to enclose tracts of land as hunting parks. It is as a result of the efforts of the Grey family in this direction that Bradgate Park was created. The rights that the people of Leicester enjoyed in the Royal Forest were strictly controlled, but included some customary privileges such as that to gather fallen wood for fuel.

A local festival which survived until the mid-18th Century was the Mock Hunting of the Hare. The festival is almost certainly evidence that the corporation of Leicester claimed some hunting rights in the former Royal Forest. When the Leicester Forest was sold off to raise money by Charles I in the 1620s, Leicester Corporation made great efforts to retain their rights and privileges.

Here is how the Hunting of the Hare was described in 1767 by an eye-witness,

"It had long before been customary, on Easter Monday, for the Mayor and his brethren, in their scarlet gowns, attended by their proper officers, in form, to go to a certain close (field), called Black-Annis' Bower Close, parcel of, or bordering upon Leicester Forest, to see the diversion of hunting, or rather the trailing of a cat before a

Leicester Town Waits
(Leicester Mercury)

pack of hounds: a custom, perhaps arising out of a claim to the royalty of the forest. Hither on a fair day, resorted the young and old, and those of all denominations. In the greatest harmony the spring was welcomed. The morning was spent in various amusements and athletic exercises, till a dead cat, about noon, was prepared by aniseed water, for commencing the mock hunting of the hare. In about half an hour, after the cat had been trailed at the tail of a horse over the grounds, in zig-zag directions the hounds were directed to the spot where the cat had been trailed from. Here the hounds gave tongue in glorious concert. The people from the various eminences, who had placed themselves to behold the sight, with shouts of rapture gave applause; the horsemen dashing after the hounds through foul passages and over fences, were emulous for taking the lead of their fellows. It was a scene, upon the whole of joy, the governing and the governed in the habits of freedom, enjoying together an innocent and recreating amusement, serving to unite them in bonds of mutual friendship, rather than to embitter their days with discord and disunion. As the cat had been trailed to the Mayor's door, through some of the principle streets, consequently the dogs and horsemen followed. After the hunt was over, the Mayor gave a handsome treat to his friends; in this manner the day was ended."

Amongst those who are mentioned as attending in their scarlet robes would have been the Town Waits in order to provide musical entertainment. The original function of the Town Waits ("Wait" derives from an Anglo-Saxon word for watchmen) was to chant the hours during the night, or to raise the alarm in case of fire. They developed however into municipal musicians, and in this role in Victorian times were responsible for singing carols in the town at Christmas time.

In 1524, the Waits had their liveries paid for from Town funds to the tune of 16 shillings (80p),

and in 1582, the Borough records show that the Aldermen each had to pay 12 pence (5p), and the Councillors 6 pence (2p) every quarter towards the Waits' wages. The Waits enjoyed a monopoly status for the provision of entertainment at weddings within the Borough, where extra cash could be earned, as well as at civic functions.

The practice of the Waits earning extra cash led to many disagreements, both between the Waits themselves, and collectively with the Corporation. They were dismissed en masse (there were five at the time) in 1601 due to internal wrangles and although four were appointed in 1603, various problems caused the dismissal of the Waits on several occasions up to 1697, when even those appointed that year were threatened with dismissal almost immediately for neglecting their duties. During the 18th century there appear to have been no disputes, whilst the Waits had their stringed instruments replaced by woodwind.

Following the municipal reform of 1835, the Waits were disbanded once again, although revived again later in the century for short periods before Christmas for the previously mentioned carol singing. The Waits finally left the Leicester scene in the early 1950s.

Another local festival was the annual "Hay Strewing" ceremony at Braunstone and Glenfield churches. At Braunstone church, the ceremony was held on the first Sunday after the feast of St Peter. On the Thursday previous to the Sunday, the hay was mown in one of the meadows on the far side of the River Soar at St Mary's Mills.

Then on the Saturday, the Parish Clerk of Braunstone fetched a small load of hay from the meadow, which on the Sunday he spread on the floor of the Church, traditionally using only his hands and without the use of a fork. Until about 1600, when grass began to be sown as a crop in its own right for the feeding of animals, hay was a very important crop, and one which was grown on a restricted amount of land. Keeping animals alive during the winter was difficult. Until the arrival of crops such as swedes and turnips from 1600 onwards, only a restricted number of cattle, sufficient to breed from the following spring could be kept alive on the meagre supplies of hay conserved from the meadows.

Meadows were usually low lying areas of grass which were too wet to be cultivated, and which gained in fertility from being flooded. The flooding also kept the ground warmer, encouraging the grass to start growing earlier in the spring and thus maximising the crop of hay which could be cut in July. A Parish would normally expect to have meadows within its own boundaries. This would usually be one large field, each farmer in the parish would have the right to the hay from a certain area, usually a strip marked by a stone. It was usual to set aside a particular part of a meadow for hay for the church. Often an individual, the church warden for example, was given the right to a portion of meadow on condition that he supplied hay for the church once a year.

What we are seeing at Braunstone was the right of the parish of Braunstone to hay from fields outside the parish boundary. Extra-parochial rights of this type were quite common. During the eighteenth century, the records tell us the hay was taken in a straight line from the meadow to the church at Braunstone. This necessitated crossing fields, ditches, hedges etc, and was made the occasion for a boisterous procession from the Soar to the church. A similar custom was enacted at the nearby church at Glenfield.

Another now defunct celebration, peculiar to Leicester, although related to similar customs in other towns, is that known as the "Whipping Toms". This was held annually on Shrove Tuesday, the last day before the forty days of the Lenten Fast, described more fully in the discussion of Easter itself. However as with so many festivals, the actual pattern of the activities is derived from several sources.

We are probably more aware of Shrove Tuesday now as "Pancake Day". The day before Shrove Tuesday used to be known as "Collop Monday", and the four days from the preceding Saturday until the Tuesday evening were marked by general feasting and high jinks. So much so that a writer in England in the seventeenth century described it as a time of

"such boiling and broiling, such roasting and toasting, such stewing and brewing, such baking, frying, mincing, cutting, carving, devouring, and gorbellied gormandising, that a man would think people did take in two months' provisions at once into their paunches, or that they did ballast their bellies with meat for a voyage to Constantinople, or the West Indies."

"Collops" refers to collops or cuts of meat, and the Monday was the time when the household meat was finished up, as no meat was allowed to be eaten during Lent. Pancakes were made in order to finish up the stocks of animal fat, also forbidden during the Lenten Fast. The ingredients of pancakes were seen to have their own special symbolism, eggs represented creation, flour was the staff of life, salt stood for wholesomeness, and milk for purity.

On the Continent of course, the period before Shrove Tuesday was the time of Carnival, culminating with Mardi Gras processions. The English climate does not lend itself to this type of celebration in late winter. A major part of the Carnival season across Europe was the inclusion of competitive games or sports, such things as horse races, running races etc. In England Shrove Tuesday was very often the time for ball games, often of a prolonged and violent nature.

Both Association Football and Rugby Football evolved from these riotous ad hoc ball games, which date back certainly to medieval times, and which often involved opposing teams from two villages. The small town of Atherstone, on the border between Leicestershire and Warwickshire is still the scene of a rough and tumble game involving a 3lb ball, the winning team being the one which has hold of the ball at the end of the day. Pubs now provide the teams, but at one time there were just two teams, one from Warwickshire and one from Leicestershire. A similar event is the annual bottle kicking at Hallaton which still takes place every Easter Monday. Two men abreast carrying sacks full of hare pies, and three men carrying aloft a 'bottle' each, two of which are filled with beer and the third being a wooden dummy, lead a procession followed by the villagers. On arrival at 'Hare-Pie Bank', an old earthwork about a quarter of a mile south of the village, the pies are tipped out of the sacks and scrambled for by the crowd. The bottles are then thrown into a circular hollow in the bank, and the men of Hallaton and the neighbouring village of Medbourne try to carry the bottles over the brook which forms the parish boundary.

These contests were once common throughout England, and are associated with boundary demarcations between two communities. The venue for the "Whipping Toms" was The Newarke. The name is a corruption of Earl Henry's "New Work", and of significance in this context is that it was an area outside the jurisdiction of the Borough of Leicester. The Newark was built by Henry of Lancaster in 1330. The actual activities were composed of two elements. Firstly two opposing teams, equipped with sticks assembled in the Newarke. At the ringing of a bell, known as the "Pancake Bell", a ball was thrown down and the two teams vied with one another to get the ball to one end of the Newarke or the other.

The "Whipping Toms" made their appearance at about one o'clock. Three men dressed in blue smocks and carrying wagon whips arrived and attempted to drive all the men and boys out of the Newarke. Whips were lashed in such a way as to try to wrap the thong around the legs of the fugitives and bring them to the ground. Some would actually challenge the "Whipping Toms" to try this, and if they were brought down they had to pay a penny forfeit. Part of the "fun" consisted of throwing missiles at poultry, some of which were tethered. It is recorded also that it was an occasion for children to play at "battledore", an early variant of badminton. The activities finally drew to a close at around five o'clock.

On one occasion in the first half of the nineteenth century, the Reverend Thomas Robinson, Vicar of St Mary's was on his way to his Vicarage which stood at the end of the Newarke, and assumed rashly that he would be immune to the attentions of the "Whipping Toms". In this he was sadly mistaken, and suffered the indignity of having to run the gauntlet of the extremely enthusiastic whippers, and finally to leap the gate into the safety of his vicarage.

Such rough forms of entertainment were falling out of favour with the Victorians. At this tine Leicester was also a major centre of Chartist activity and the authorities were particularly nervous of occasions which encouraged large crowds to gather. The annual Shrove Tuesday festivities were finally brought to an end in 1847 by an Act of Parliament. The origins of this festival lie in the separate jurisdictions. The ball game element is typical, as we have seen, of boundary rivalries, whilst the ritualised clearing out of strangers from the area of the Newarke no doubt reflects the separate jurisdictions, and in particular that the authority of the Borough, granted by Royal Charter and applying to the area inside the town walls, did not apply to the area of the Newarke.

The Crown and Thistle, recently renamed the Fourpence and Firkin, in Loseby Lane, is the scene annually on June 24th of a ceremony involving

"Whipping Toms" plaque in the Newarke (Leicester City Council)

the pub landlord, the Mayor, members of the Guild of Freemen and the Town Crier. The landlord calls the Mayor to the pub to receive the annual rent of four old pennies and a damask rose. The land on which the pub now stands at one time formed part of the land of the former Hospital of St Mary, built during the 14th Century, and endowed by Henry, Duke of Lancaster.

The ownership of this land passed to the Borough of Leicester in 1614. The origin of this annual ceremony is the sale of the land, by the Borough, in 1636. The price paid was forty shillings, plus the annual rent of four pence and the rose, which was the symbol of the Duchy of Lancaster. The presence of the rose as part of the annual rent probably recalls a pledge of loyalty to the house of Lancaster as part of the conditions of the original lease.

One of the ways in which we all participate in festivals is by sending greetings cards to one another. The first greetings cards were for Valentine's Day. Valentine's Day is one of those festivals which the church made strenuous efforts to suppress but failed. The day has its origins in the Roman spring festival of Lupercalia.

There, the names of young ladies were placed in a box, to be draw out by young men, who thus chose their partner for the festivities. One can see why such a process could have its adherents, and why the celebrations refused to die! The Church's bright idea of replacing the names of the young ladies with those of saints, to whom one then offered prayers did not quite have the same attraction and was something of a non-starter. This was carried out on the feast of St Valentine, who thus bequeathed the name, but left the motives intact.

Over the centuries the practice changed somewhat. In 1661, Samuel Pepys the diarist tells us that one's Valentine for the day was the first person to be met on February the 14th. Pepys, something of a philanderer, contrived to meet the person of his choice, as no doubt did most other people. Letters were also written on this day from one `Valentine' to another. By around 1750, carefully designed and coloured Valentine cards, hand made at home, were being sent. The custom spread during the 1780s and 1790s.

By 1800, they were being produced commercially in the form of embossed stationery printed with loving couplets. The arrival of the universal penny post in 1840, and the growing use of envelopes to provide privacy (original Valentines sent through the post were folded in half and postmarked on the back) provided the impetus for a rapidly growing custom and industry.

A forerunner of the modern Kissagram was to send a hamper to the door of the loved one out of which would spring a young boy dressed as Cupid - decorum ruled for the Victorians! The cards became ever more elaborate, decorated with lace, silk, gold leaf etc.

Valentines were not always meant to be taken seriously, and there is a long tradition of sending anonymous cards, sometimes humorous, as illustrated by the following excerpt from the Living History Unit's publication "The Diary of Ada Jackson 1883" shows:

"Mother had a valentine today, they judge me of sending it, they won't believe me when I say I did not. I suppose G. had an ugly one too. I wonder who sent it... I did not have a valentine but I am not disappointed as I did not expect one, I have still got the glamour of love over my eyes." (G. was Ada's boyfriend.)

Cards for Mother's Day and Father's Day are a much more recent custom. Mothering Sunday has long been celebrated in England on the fourth Sunday in Lent. The origin of the festival was as the day that a visit was made to worship at the Church in one's parish of birth, i.e. an individual's "Mother Church". As this usually meant a return to the location where one's parents, and particularly mother still lived, the day became associated with the recording of thanks to one's mother.

Until early this century, one of the most important sources of employment for the young was to "enter service". This entailed leaving home to work in a domestic capacity in somebody's home. The use of domestic servants was more widespread than usually realised, and surprisingly humble households could employ such labour. For many young people employed in this fashion, Mothering Sunday was one of the few opportunities to return home, and could well be the only one.

Valentine's Day card c 1920 (Leicester City Council)

The day was marked by special church services and also certain special foods, notably "frumenty", a concoction of wheat grains boiled in milk with added sugar and spices, and Simnel cake. Recipes for Simnel cake vary from region to region, but it is basically a very rich fruit cake.

The growth of both Mother's Day and Father's Day as major Greetings Card festivals are however the result of developments in America over the last hundred years. In America, Mother's Day (celebrated there on the second Sunday in May, note the different name and the fixed date) was the work of Miss Anna Jarvis of Philadelphia. Miss Jarvis' mother departed this life on the 9th May 1906, and shortly after Miss Jarvis announced to the world that she would commemorate the death of her mother by a day devoted to Mothers everywhere.

If Miss Jarvis had only first consulted the local church regarding a suitable date, she might have saved some multinational greetings card companies some of their marketing problems. One can only marvel however at the indefatigable efforts of Miss Jarvis, who bombarded senators, congressmen, state governments with an absolute welter of mail imploring them, shaming them, and cajoling them into naming this as Mother's Day. Of her success there can be no doubt, and it was not long before the American greetings card industry was making handsome profits from her crusade.

In the UK, mothers continued to be honoured in the traditional way, with a visit home by dutiful sons and daughters and a special service at the parish church.

This is an elderly resident of Leicester describing a Mothering Sunday service from her childhood,

"We went to Sunday School, and on Sunday mornings after we had been in Sunday School we went into church for the main service, but we were allowed to creep out when it came time for the sermon, because they thought it was a little bit too boring for the young people. On Mothering Sunday it was beautiful and it was something I'd really like to go and see again. The church was so full they had to put chairs in the aisles for this particular service. What happened was the Sunday before we wrote out a card to our mother, and on Mothering Sunday our teacher gave us each a bunch of usually violets, and if not violets, daffodils, and our mothers came and lined a path that led up to the church on either side of the path. We came out of one door and round and as you came to your mother, you gave her your flowers, and she joined in the procession back into the church. Oh the violets! And to see your mother standing there. There was no `you go this way and you go that way'... everybody knew exactly what to do. It was a really lovely service."

It was the arrival of American servicemen here during the war that really gave an impetus to the habit of sending greetings cards to one's Mother. The date chosen for this however was the traditional English Mothering Sunday rather than the American Mothers Day. During the last few years the total of cards sent nationwide for Mothers Day has exceeded 35 million each year.

Fathers Day had a very similar genesis. It commemorates the death of a mother during the American Civil War. The father continued to bring up the children, and after they left home, continued to write to their father annually to commemorate the death of their mother and their father's continued commitment to the family. Dating from June 9th, 1910, this is the day now celebrated as Fathers Day, once again first introduced here by American Service personnel during the second world war, but promoted heavily by the greetings card companies ever since.

One relatively recent "manufactured" festival which has come and gone is Empire Day. This festival, created to celebrate all that was great and noble about the British Empire was fixed on May 24th, Queen Victoria's birthday.

The British Empire has gone, replaced by the Commonwealth. Here, however, is how an octogenarian citizen of Leicester remembers Empire Day from her schooldays,

"We always assembled out in the school yard, each class had its own line. We were inspected for shoes, (finger)nails, and to have a clean handkerchief. The headmistress came down one file and went up another and then we all went in for assembly. On Empire Day, the door that we used to go through to the assembly hall was draped with a huge Union Jack, and as we went through we had to bow to the flag, and that went on until all the children were assembled. It was made an awful lot of in those days. We were very patriotic, we were taught to be patriotic."

Empire Day has disappeared from the calendar. Attempts were made, however, to prolong it by changing the name to Commonwealth Day.

It has been mentioned several times that the Puritan revolution and the establishment of the Commonwealth under Oliver Cromwell was responsible for attempted suppression of Christmas and other festivals. The restoration of the monarchy under Charles II in 1660 saw the start of a celebratory day on May 29th. Known as Oak Apple Day, recalling his hiding in an oak tree to escape capture, observance of it clung on till this century. Into the 1890s, trains on the Manchester, Sheffield and Lincolnshire Railway were decorated with branches of oak to mark the day. Some of Leicester's residents can remember other ways of celebrating the day,

"Oak Apple Day! If you hadn't got a sprig of oak, the boys used to come with nettles and nettle your legs! You made sure you'd got your oak leaves pinned on, of course we wore short socks, or you got your legs nettled with the boys!"

We have seen how festivals have evolved around the patterns of economic existence, from hunter gatherers to agriculturalists. The last change was to the festivals of an industrial economy. Attention has been drawn to the way in which the Victorians suppressed those festivals which were considered unruly, such as the Whipping Toms.

That this was in part the result of changes in what was considered acceptable behaviour may be judged by the following description of the Whipping Toms in the 1820s,

"...a scene of gaiety and humour to which the young look forward with considerable animation...", and again, *"... a scene of considerable mirth."*

Yet just twenty years after that was written, the Whipping Toms were being abolished by the Leicester Improvement Act of 1846. Many at the time bemoaned the end of such "traditional" customs. Here is a commentator writing a year or two before the Whipping Toms were abolished,

"What a revolution of taste has taken place in the English people... The times, and the spirit of the times are changed: we are no longer merry England, but busy England; England full of wealth and poverty - extravagance and care. There has been no small lamentation over this change; and many of our writers have laboured hard to bring us once more to adopt this state of things. They might as well attempt to bring back jousts and tourneys, popery, and government without representation."

The factory based manufacturing economy imposed a discipline on time which did not allow for such frivolity. This discipline is breaking down. People's patterns of work are becoming far more diverse as more and more become self- employed or work from home. Legislation leading to liberalisation of Sunday shopping both reflects this trend and encourages it. This process is likely to be enhanced in Leicester, where around a quarter of the population derive from a non-Christian background.

Christmas of course continues to dominate as the festival of the year. It has just as great an impact on non-Christians due to the enormous commercial pressures it generates, as well as the enforced changes to work patterns. For the majority of people however it is the customs of Christmas, from the office party to the family lunch on Christmas Day which have as great a significance as the celebrations of the birth of Christ.

Apart from providing a framework for the year, festivals perform other vital functions within the community. We have seen that they are a time for "letting your hair down". A time when social barriers, even though temporarily, are broken down. They are also a time when all members of the community act together in the pursuit of a common goal. If these functions are being lost by traditional festivals is there any sign that something else may replace them?

This is a subject of great relevance as far as Leicester is concerned because of the multi-ethnic nature of the city. Whilst the most committed Christian, Muslim, Sikh, Jew or Hindu may send greetings or even join in the festivals of other faiths they will never have the meaning that they do to the individuals whose festival it is.

As we have seen, festivals have a role to play in the pride of a community in itself. Carnival is when you can be yourself, and re-enforce your pride in the uniqueness of being African-Caribbean. Festivals may either be celebrated uniquely and exclusively by the cultural group concerned, or efforts may be made to use participation in festivals, across cultural boundaries, to promote understanding and awareness.

Whilst the first of these alternatives may ensure cultural purity and continuance, the second is likely to lead to a far more harmonious community, although with the penalty of

compromise, and the acceptance of the notion that cultures have to change and adapt themselves to the strictures of the times, and the needs of the communities' members. The history of all the festivals celebrated in Leicester over the last two thousand years shows us that change is indeed inevitable.

The history of festivals is one of evolution. Cultures procreate and adapt festivals so they are relevant to their needs - to celebrate the coming of the seasons, the birth of a religious leader and so on. The world's great religions, Christianity, Islam, Judaism, Hinduism and Sikhism are all intimately connected with books, and with the writing down of wisdom and commandments.

To look for parallels in the modern world, we must start to look at events generated by the media of today. More and more, we share our experiences through the medium of television. The BBC's Children in Need Appeal, for instance, fulfils all the criteria by which festivals may be defined. It re-occurs every year, it touches in some way or another virtually everybody in the country, it breaks down social barriers, and through the medium of the various fund-raising events, it encourages a suspension of day to day behaviour. This latter characteristic is even more marked on the similar Red Nose Day.

Festivals such as these can have a unifying effect. As they are non-religious in nature they appeal to all cultural groups within the city, and particularly to the young. Great sporting festivals such as the Olympic games fulfil much the same role on an international level, again with television as the mediating agent. We have yet to see the same theme developing at a city level. It is true of course that Children in Need, or Red Nose Day call for organisation at a local level.

As electronics more and more become the accepted method of national and international communication, we can expect the same to happen at a local level. Could it be that the key to future local festivals in Leicester lies with all those trenches being dug under the pavements throughout the city? Local television, which from the start has been designed to be interactive, could be where Leicester's electronic festivals of the future will take place.

Indeed, local radio in Leicester is already starting to fulfil this role. By 1994, Carnival Radio was an important part of the African-Caribbean Carnival proceedings. Plans were also announced that for Diwali and Navratri a similar provision was to be made.

Attention has been drawn to the suspension of normal day to day activities as one of the key characteristics of a festival, often as time away from normal work. It is this time away from normal activities which allows the time for the celebrations, rituals and cultural activity of the festival. Without this time, the festival becomes eroded and gradually loses its richness and variety.

This suspension of normal activity is most important for the children. This is when the beliefs and practices of a culture are handed on to new generations. One of the recurring themes mentioned by representatives Leicester's ethnic groups was the importance of bequeathing the children the cultural identity implicit in the celebration of a festival. Above all was the feeling that because, Diwali, Eid and Baisakhi were normal working days the importance of them was gradually being reduced.

As we have seen, festivals act as a kind of community cement, binding the members of a community together. If all the citizens of Leicester were free to take part in the respective celebrations it would surely increase mutual understanding and tolerance, whilst at the same time ensuring that the meaning of the festival was passed on to the children. A possible start to this could be by marking Eid, Diwali and Baisakhi as public holidays throughout the city - some employers having already started in this direction.

Appendix

THE DIVISION OF TIME

Festivals are intimately bound up with the division of time.
Based on the observable movements of the sun and the moon,
different cultures have produce different methods of dividing
up time. A SOLAR month is one twelfth of a solar year,
approximately 30 days. A LUNAR month is the time it takes
for the moon to make one complete journey around the earth
and is approximately 29 days. Given that a day is always one
complete period of light and dark, the period of the lunar
cycle, the lunar month, is the next most convenient division
of time. During each lunar month, the moon passes through
several phases, indicated by its shape as seen by an observer
on Earth. In reality of course it always remains spherical.

At the start of each lunar cycle, the moon is described as "new", at this time it is almost invisible, but after a day or two assumes the shape of a thin crescent seen in the western sky. It gradually grows larger, until at the end of the first "quarter", half of the disk is visible. The amount of the moon illuminated by the sun continues to grow to the end of the second quarter, when the whole of its disk is visible. The moon is then described as a "full" moon. From the point at which it first becomes visible to the time of the full moon, it is described as waxing. The second two quarters, as the amount of the visible disk grows smaller, it is said to be waning.

Twelve lunar cycles amount to 354 days, eleven and a quarter days less than a solar year. The ways in which different peoples have arranged their calendars all represent different solutions to the problem of this eleven and a quarter days, and how to reconcile lunar months of 29 days with a solar month which is one twelfth of the solar year and consists of roughly 30 days.

The Jewish Calendar is a lunar calendar. Whilst the year is divided into 12 months, the lengths of the months are all either 29 or 30 days, the time of the lunar cycle being 29 days. The Jewish year therefore contains 354 days, eleven days less than the solar year. The anomaly is resolved by inserting an extra month known as Adar Sheni, or Adar 2, seven times over a nineteen year period.

This prevents festivals which are associated with particular seasons of the year, such as Passover, a spring festival, from gradually moving to an inappropriate time of the year. The flexibility within the calendar also allows anomalies, such as the coincidence of a fast day with the Sabbath, to be avoided. The numbering of Jewish years commences at a date which corresponds to 3,760 BC. Jewish days begin at sunset, and not at midnight.

The Islamic calendar, also a lunar calendar, makes no attempt to reconcile the lunar year with the solar year. The Islamic year consists of 12 months consisting of 29 or 30 days resulting in a year of 354 days, 11 days short of a solar year of 365 days. There still remains a slight discrepancy which is resolved by the addition of a day in each of eleven years of a thirty year period. These eleven years are thus leap years of 355 days.

The actual start of an Islamic month depends upon an actual sighting of the new moon on the evening of the 29th day of a month. If the new moon is sighted, that evening marks the start of the next month. If the new moon is not sighted on the evening of the 29th day, the first day of the month is automatically assumed to start the evening of the following day. This means that all published dates of Muslim festivals according to the western calendar are approximate.

It is easy, when applying the appellation Hindu, to think of India as an homogeneous culture. Nothing could be further from the truth. The Indian sub-continent is a disparate collection of peoples, cultures and landscapes, and Hinduism is more rightly thought of as a collection of faiths held together by certain underlying beliefs, institutions and practices.

This variety is echoed by the Hindu calendar. There are actually two major Hindu calendars, both modified by different traditions and each displaying local variations. Both calendars consist of twelve lunar months. One calendar calculates the start of the month from the moment of the full moon, the other from the start of the new moon. To cause further complications, both systems call the months by the same names, although here again there are regional differences.

There are also twelve parallel solar months, whose names coincide with the familiar astrological constellations, with the exception of Capricorn (The Goat), which is replaced by Makara (The Crocodile). The start and finish of a solar day is at sunrise and not at midnight as in the western calendar.

In order to bring the Hindu calendars into accord with the solar year, months are added, or very occasionally, deleted. Basically an additional month appears in the calendar every two to three years, normally after Ashadha (June/July) or Shravana (July/August). The additional month bears the name of the month immediately preceding it, prefixed by the word 'second', i.e. second Ashadha and so on.

It is possible for communities from different parts of India to be inconsistent with this process, which can mean festivals being celebrated on different dates. This happened in 1982, when Leicester's Gujarati Hindu communities celebrated Diwali at a different time to Punjabi Sikhs and Hindus. There are also divergences in the date marking the start of a new year. In Gujarat, the new year starts in Kartikka (October/November), the month when Diwali is celebrated, which thus for Gujaratis is a New Year Festival. Other parts of India, significantly for Leicester the Punjab, traditionally start the New Year in the month of Chaitra (March/April).

There are also different methods of numbering years according to different starting dates. The Indian National Calendar uses a start date which corresponds to 78 AD. Importantly, Hindu months are divided into two fortnights, or pakshas. The first fortnight is the "bright half" or shukla-paksha, often abbreviated to sud, and corresponds to the waxing time of the new moon to the full moon.

The "dark half" or krishnapaksha (vad) corresponds to the period when the moon is waning, i.e. from full moon to new moon. The very fact that the word "fortnight" (it is a contraction of "fourteen nights") exists in the English language is almost certainly evidence of a similar long forgotten division of the lunar month.

The Chinese have also employed a lunar calendar for most of their long history. The year is divided into twelve lunar months of 29 or 30 days each. The formulators of the calendar, which dates from the Shang dynasty (1765-1123 BC), understood from the start that their year of 354 days would not correspond to the solar year, and therefore added an extra month once every three years. Interestingly, they also named the days in a sixty day cycle, and the years similarly. The current sixty year cycle commenced in 1984.

The years are associated with twelve animals corresponding to the twelve signs of the zodiac, the names following one and other in a set order. The Chinese New Year always falls on the day of the first new moon after the sun enters Aquarius. The date always falls between 21st January and 20th February in the western calendar.

The older Chinese peasant festivals betray their agricultural origins with names such as the "Waking of Insects", and "Grain in the Ear". The principle festival celebrated by Leicester's Chinese and Vietnamese (who share the same festival) communities is the Chinese New Year.

The familiar western calendar is derived from the Roman calendar, and is a purely solar calendar. The calendar was revised and corrected by Julius Caesar in 45 BC, and henceforth was known as the Julian Calendar, but even this had accumulated an error of 10 days by 1582. In that year, Pope Gregory XIII ruled that the 5th October should be the 15th October, in order to remove the ten day error.

The Catholic countries of Europe went along with this, but the Protestant countries did not. The Netherlands and Germany for instance did not adopt the Gregorian calendar until 1700, whilst it was not until 1752 that England swung into line and the 3rd September that year became the 14th, the accumulated error by then having become eleven days.

Other countries and cultures, who also used the Gregorian calendar did not bring their calendars into line with the reformed calendar until later. It was 1918, for instance before it was adopted by Russia, and it was not accepted by the Greek orthodox church until 1924.

The number of days in each month of the Gregorian calendar is fixed in order to arrive at an annual total of 365 days, just a quarter day short of the actual 365 and a quarter days which it takes for the earth to make one journey around the sun. The quarter day short is reconciled by the insertion of an extra day in February every four years. The year with an extra day is known as a Leap Year.

The commencement for the numbering of years usually depends on a significant event within the culture. For Islam, this significant date is the time when the Prophet Mohammed and his followers left Mecca and journeyed across the desert to Medina. In the western calendar this occurred in 622 AD. To Muslims however this was year one. The year this is being written is 1994 AD (an abbreviation of Anno Domini in Latin which translates as the "Year of Our Lord") in the western calendar. For the Islamic world, year 1414

AH, which started during 1993 will become year 1415 AH on the 10th August 1994. (the letters AH refer to Anno or After Hijrah. The Hijrah is the name given to the Prophet Mohammed's journey from Mecca to Medina).

As we saw above, the Muslim year, being based on lunar months is 11 days shorter than the western year. This means that every thirty-three years, the Muslim calendar appears to lose a year when compared to the western calendar. This may be thought to be of purely academic interest, but for Muslims living in countries using the Gregorian calendar it results in practical difficulties.

The most immediate effect is that Muslim festivals appear to move backwards each year by eleven days. For Muslims living in northern climes however this acquires even greater significance. The major festival for Muslims is Ramadan. One of the principle articles of the Muslim faith is that during Ramadan, between dawn and dusk, no food or water should pass one's lips.

If Ramadan were to start, for example, on the 1st January one year it would start on the 20th December the next, the 9th December the next and so on. Gradually moving backwards until after sixteen years it would be occurring six months earlier in June. A period of fasting which is around 10 hours when Ramadan occurs in an English winter, theoretically extends to around 17 hours when Ramadan occurs in June.

The use of the letters AD in the western calendar are starting to be replaced by the letters CE. The letters standing for Common Era. Similarly BC is being replaced by BCE for Before Common Era. One can perhaps see some sense in removing the Christian element from a calendar which is fast becoming a world calendar, although it would have gained rather more credence if the numbering of the years had started afresh. Use of the BCE suffix means that the calendar is still firmly nailed to the Christian method of reckoning.

SEASONAL RITUALS - THE START OF FESTIVALS

Anthropologists explain the start of seasonal rituals in terms of the tensions created within primitive societies as the seasonal transition points of the year were approached. Primitive societies explained the world around them by a system which supposed that all things, vegetable, animal, inanimate objects and features in the landscape possessed their own souls or spirits. This also applied to the sun, the moon and the natural elements such as the wind and the rain.

At points in time when a certain sequence of events was expected of the elements or animal populations, rituals developed to encourage the spirit living within the wind, the rain, the sun or the moon, or the spirit of the caribou, to behave as was expected.

Those whose lives became intimately bound with one species of animal, like the Lapps and their reindeer today, would have become used to annual migrations to follow the herds in response to the different seasons. Almost certainly the cave paintings of France and Spain are evidence of rituals connected with the hunting of animals for food. Many of the paintings are concerned with success in the chase.

Others paintings however voice another concern. Not only were the hunters looking for successful hunts, but they had realised that they needed a sufficient quantity of animals to hunt. In order for there to be a sufficient food supply, there needed to be a successful breeding season. The pictures of animals apparently pregnant suggest that here we have physical evidence illustrating the beginnings of seasonal festivals.

It is from this time, twenty thousand years ago, that what appear to be the first calendars date. Bones carved with a series of marks which reflect the shape of the moon as it moves through the month have been found together with others which have been notched in a regular pattern which seem to be a record of days.

The connection between the height of the sun above the horizon and the seasonal progression would also have become apparent. The higher the sun rises the warmer the days become. The regularity with which this happens every year would have been noted, as would the regularity of the phases of the moon. It would have been noticed too that the stars also appear to move in a regular fashion.

As humankind moved from being a hunter to the more settled life of a farmer, the pattern of the year became ever more important. When to plough, when to sow, when to reap were crucial decisions, decisions which if incorrect led to hunger. The association between the sun, the seasons and an abundant harvest could hardly fail to bring about firstly a mechanism to predict when the rains would come, and hence when to plough and to sow, and following that a process by which the timing or the reliability of the seasonal procession could be influenced. The mechanisms which saw the development of calendars to divide and measure the passage of time, and yearly rituals to influence the seasons or celebrate the fruits of harvest were in place.

One place which was more exposed to seasonal variation than any other was ancient Egypt. Egypt is a land of almost perpetual summer and no rain. Egyptian agriculture depended, and still does, entirely on the Nile for a water supply, and hence for the fertility of the soil. By May, the Nile dwindles to little more than a trickle. From June onwards, fed by melting snows in the mountains of Abyssinia and the heavy African rains it grows steadily, inundating the land to either side and bringing with it a layer of fertile alluvium, washed from the mountainsides down which it cascades.

The Egyptians were interested observers of the heavens. They noticed that Sirius the Dog Star rose just before the Sun on the day that the inundation started. This day was designated as New Years Day and became the basis for an artificial calendar of 365 days divided into 12 months. This calendar is believed to have started in 4241 BC, thus making it the earliest fixed date in human history.

A common feature to all festivals is that they are regularly periodic, and normally annual, i.e. celebrated at the same time each year. However this regularity depends upon the different ways which different cultures have developed for keeping track of time. A further complication is that the length of a year can be different for different societies. The mechanism for dividing and describing time for longer periods than 24 hours is the calendar, and to understand the timing of the various festivals which are or have been celebrated in Leicester, we need an appreciation of these different methods of arranging time.

A solar year is the time it takes for the earth to make one complete journey around the sun. Due to the tilt of the earth, the progress of the year in the northern hemisphere is perceived as the sun rising higher and higher in the sky each day after the winter solstice. The winter solstice which falls on 21 December marks the lowest point which the sun reaches as it rises above the horizon (technically it is when the sun is overhead at the Tropic of Capricorn, the furthest south that it appears to move).

The winter solstice is therefore the day with shortest daylight and longest night. The summer solstice, which falls on 21 June, celebrated as Midsummers Day in the northern hemisphere, is the day with the longest daylight and shortest night, when the sun is overhead at the Tropic of Cancer. From this time onwards the days start to shorten once more.

The spring and autumn equinoxes are the two intermediate days between the solstices, when night-time and daylight are equal. In the southern hemisphere, the times of the winter and summer solstices are reversed, however most people living in Leicester today originated in countries to the North of the Equator. The actual time for a complete cycle is approximately 365 days. The spring or vernal equinox falls on 21 March, and the autumn equinox on 23 September. The solstices and the equinoxes have played a significant role in the development of many festivals which are celebrated today.

FIXING THE DATE OF EASTER

Easter is a movable festival, that is it does not return on the same day every year. The reason for this is that the time of its celebration derives from the date of the Jewish festival of the Passover, which is calculated according to the Jewish, lunar, calendar. The calculation of the date is based on references in the Gospels (Mark, Ch. 14; Luke, Ch. 22; Matthew Ch. 24) that the gathering of the disciples for the Last Supper was on "the first day of unleavened bread when they sacrificed the Passover".

The calculation of Easter caused some major problems in the early English church. When Saint Augustine and his followers arrived they brought with them what had become the standard Catholic method of calculating Easter which is still used. This in itself had only been arrived at after bitter disputes within the early church, disputes which had provided one of the main reasons for the split between the eastern and western branches of Christianity. The debate raged around whether the Resurrection should be marked always on a Sunday, or on whichever day of the week the appropriate day of the Passover was to be celebrated.

For those who would like to reckon the date for themselves, Easter Sunday falls on the first Sunday after the full moon which falls on or after the 21st day of March (the Spring Equinox). In the event of the full moon occurring on a Sunday, Easter Sunday is the next Sunday after. Simple. However when Augustine's mission from Rome arrived on these shores, as they and their successors pushed northwards, converting as they went, they eventually came into contact with Celtic Christianity which had continued in Wales, Scotland and Ireland after the departure of the Romans.

The Celtic Church calculated Easter in a different fashion. We may be amused at this distance in time to learn that in the court of the Northumbrian Royal Family in the 7th Century, the Queen kept to the Celtic Easter and the King to the Roman. In 631 AD this led to the King celebrating Easter Sunday, having finished his lenten fast, whilst the Queen and her followers were celebrating Palm Sunday, which occurs a week before Easter Sunday, and were still observing their fast for lent! The church, however was not amused, and the differences were not resolved in Britain until the Council of Whitby in 664 AD which slowly but eventually led to a harmonisation of the calculation of the date. All the moveable feasts in the Christian calendar are dependant on Easter for their calculation.

The early development of Christianity of course took place within a Jewish setting. Early Christians continued to keep the Festival of Passover as they had always done. Paul, one of the first Christian evangelists, was not a Jew. He built upon the symbolism of the passover feast however, and placed it within a Christian context, in his first letter to the Corinthians (Ch.5 v. 7 and following). Here he refers to Christ as a sacrificial lamb for everyone's sins, and goes on to state that Christians should keep the feast with "the unleavened bread of sincerity and truth".